If Not
"Pre-Trib Rapture,"
Then What?

Teri Sue Riddering, TH.D.

WESTBOW
PRESS®
A DIVISION OF THOMAS NELSON
& ZONDERVAN

WestBow Press books may be ordered through booksellers or by contacting:

WestBow Press
A Division of Thomas Nelson & Zondervan
1663 Liberty Drive
Bloomington, IN 47403
www.westbowpress.com
1 (866) 928-1240

ISBN: 978-1-9736-7707-9 (sc)
ISBN: 978-1-9736-7706-2 (e)

Print information available on the last page.

WestBow Press rev. date: 1/06/2020

Contents

Introduction ix

Chapter 1   Why Should we Worry about Correct Eschatology?....1

Chapter 2   Brief Eschatological History of the Church.................5

Chapter 3   Quick Summary of Main Premillennial Theories 13

    A. Pretribulational "Rapture"...13

    B. Midtribulational "Rapture"...15

    C. Postribulational "Rapture" 16

Chapter 4   Contentions with the Pretribulational Rapture
                 Theory 19

    A. Questioning its origins 19

    B. Questioning its hermeneutics...24

    C. Replacement and/or Dual Covenant theologies...............33

    D. Problems with prophetic timing...38

Chapter 5   Correct Christian and Jewish Hermeneutical
                 Practices...45

Chapter 6   Fundamental Principles to the Eschatological
                 Jigsaw Puzzle 53

A. Four "Corners" of the Puzzle.............................57

   1. God's OT saints and present-day Jews are still
      God's people..58

   2. The Church is included in God's New Covenant
      with Israel...59

   3. God has partially fulfilled His promises
      regarding Israel's land..................................59

   4. God will keep His promises of resurrection and
      the Kingdom. 60

B. Four "Sides" of the Puzzle 61

   1. Resurrection of New Covenant Saints
      (1st Resurrection) 61

   2. Messianic Millennial Kingdom 62

   3. Judgment of Unbelievers (2nd Resurrection)..............62

   4. The Father's Eternal Kingdom (New Heaven
      and New Earth)..63

Chapter 7   Redefining Important Concepts..................65

A. Great Tribulation vs. Normal Tribulations 65

   1. Great Tribulation.......................................65

   2. Normal Tribulations, Signs, and Wrath 71

   3. Tribulations of Early Believers..................... 80

   4. Present Worldwide Tribulations...................82

B. Daniel's Final Week 88

C. God's Two Witnesses.................................. 101

   1. The two anointed ones: Israel and the Church.......... 101

   2. Jews and Christians raised out of their tribulations... 105

D. The Antichrist...106

   1. Various Historical Evil Kingdoms...........106

2. Many antichrists and false prophets 107

3. Beasts and Horns 109

4. The Beasts of Revelation.. 118

5. Man of Lawlessness still restrained 127

E. Signs of the End Times 135

1. The Seals and Trumpets of Revelation 135

2. Salvation/Redemption of Israel............................. 142

3. The Final Seventh Trumpet 151

F. Mystery of God Fulfilled... 160

1. Marriage Supper of the Lamb in Heaven 160

2. Second Beast's Dominion on Earth 164

G. Christ's Return and Final Events................................... 167

1. Parousía and Messianic Kingdom 167

2. Second Resurrection, Final Judgment, and
Father's Kingdom... 170

Chapter 8   Proposed Final Picture of the Puzzle....................... 173

Chapter 9   Common Eschatological Perspectives in
Christianity and Judaism.. 181

A. Messiah ben Joseph and Messiah ben David................... 181

B. Repentance necessary for redemption 183

C. Human atonement for sin 184

D. Unity of many Gentiles and Jews prior to resurrection ... 186

E. Personal/National resurrection, Messianic Age,
World to Come.. 187

Chapter 10 Significance of Proposed Theory 189

A. Jewish/Christian Unity through Resurrection 189

B. Final Spiritual/Cosmic Fulfillment of God's Purposes ... 193

    1. Tension between God's mercy and justice resolved ... 194

    2. Human immortality obtained in imperishable bodies 195

    3. Humanity restored to the Divine image 195

    4. God's promises fulfilled to all His people 196

Chapter 11 How Should we Respond? 197

A. Our Christian Responsibility 197

B. An Imagined Frontier 200

Appendices 203
Bibliography 217

Introduction

This book is a careful attempt to explore and "fill in the picture" of the eschatological puzzle using the entire Biblical Scripture cohesively within a conceptual framework of two peoples, Jew and Christian, His people of the New Covenant (Jer. 31:31; Matt. 2:28) united under one Messiah as *"one new man"* (Eph. 2:15). Using solid hermeneutical practices, I attempt to disprove some major aspects of the Pretribulational "Rapture" theory because it produces a distorted picture of future events regarding the relationship between Jews and Christians. I have organized prophetic past, present, and future events into a logical and coherent sequence that more closely resembles historical reality and God's eternal plans. At the end, I highlight some of the similarities between Christian and Jewish eschatologies, and then describe the final outcome of God's eternal purposes with mankind while offering some suggestions as to what Christians can do as they await victoriously for the converging of both eschatologies and for the fulfillment of all things.

In 1995, God began revealing His heart to me regarding the Jewish people and His eternal plans with Israel. He also led me to go to Israel and was able to live there among the Jewish people for a total of seven years, volunteering with an interdenominational Christian organization while at the same time learning about the Jewish perspective of Scripture and their own eschatological ideas. In

2011, I published my first book titled: ***Rising to Everlasting Life: The Resurrection Texts for both Christians and Jews***. In this book, I discuss a collection of the main Biblical and extra-Biblical texts that describe the final resurrection of the saints, comparing the Christian with the Jewish perspectives, and concluding that both are not only parallel, but identical, since we use the same Scriptures as God's revealed truth. Thus, both groups must visualize their own promised resurrection as a joint event, not leaving anyone behind, since we will ultimately form one same body in the Messiah.

Performing a rigorous investigation as objectively as possible, the above foundational premise represents the guiding light which has illuminated the analysis and theory herein proposed. I had a pretty good idea of what other theorists were proposing about this topic, but I wanted to limit this research regarding the often-times confusing pieces of the puzzle exclusively to Scripture and depend only on the Holy Spirit's guidance to place them according to God's divine order. His character and eternal purposes established the irrefutable and non-negotiable "borders" and "corners" of the puzzle as I began to fill in the picture around the main "centerpiece" of Matthew 24:29-31. After about 25 years of patient work to organize the pieces according to God's perspective, I discovered that I can agree with a few elements of all three typical Tribulational Rapture theories, but my end picture is far different from all three.

Reinterpreting Daniel's "last week" as a centuries-long extension of time rather than just seven short years, all the symbolic concepts fall into logical place. I also **avoid:** 1) a Pretribulational idea of the "rapture" for solely the Church before the "Tribulation"; 2) a Midtribulationist view of the Sixth Seal as being the "Tribulation" mid-point before the "rapture"; and 3) a Postribulational perspective of Jesus' simultaneous return *for* His saints and *with* His saints, among other things. From a positive perspective, I **incorporate**: 1) the Pretribulational idea that Christ will come *for* His saints at their resurrection as a distinct event from when He returns in glory *with* His saints at the second coming or *Parousia*, plus the global dominance of the "Antichrist" between these two events; 2) the Midtribulational understanding about the outpouring of the God's wrath only upon unbelievers following the "tribulation" and "resurrection" of the saints; and 3) the Postribulational concept of Christ's appearance "after the tribulation of those days." This perspective could be visualized as a Post-Tribulation / Pre-Wrath Rapture picture, though I prefer to call it my **"Joint Christian and Jewish Resurrection Theory."**

Thus, this book is a careful exposition of what I believe is the true Biblical vision regarding the past, present, and future of the world in relation to God Himself. I do not claim to have all the answers, but since I have begun with a solid Biblical base of who God is and what He wants to ultimately accomplish with mankind, I am confident that my picture matches more closely His final picture than the more popular theories. I pray that this may reach the hearts and minds of all those who truly seek God and His plans for the end-times.

Why Should we Worry about Correct Eschatology?

Why does it matter what we believe in regarding the end-times, or whether there is contradiction between the various Christian perspectives? Some may say, "God can do what He needs to do even if I don't know what He is doing," or "If things turn out differently than I expect, it doesn't matter." True, God will make sure that His will is fulfilled in the long run, no matter what anybody believes or understands. But what if God is waiting for His people to do certain things in order to fulfill His plan, and since we do not respond to His leading, nothing happens? What if **all** we are doing is *"waiting for our blessed hope, the appearing of the glory of our great God and Savior Jesus Christ"* (Tit 2:13), when God wants us to do something, such as praying according to His perfect will or teaching about how God wants to create "one new man" out of both Jews and Christians? It would be best if the Lord found us ready and obedient, spiritually feeding the household of God before He comes:

> *"Therefore you also must **be ready**, for the Son of Man is coming at an hour you do not expect. Who then is the faithful*

*and wise servant, whom his master has set over his household, to give them their food at the proper time? Blessed is that servant whom **his master will find so doing when he comes**"* (Matt. 24:44-46, ESV).

The Biblical study of the end-times, known as *eschatology* in the Christian academic world, is very often relegated to the back burner in most Christian environments because more "important" doctrines usually obtain priority, especially if those other subjects are perceived as being more relevant to the individual Christian and to the believing community in general. But Millard J. Erickson declared that some theologians "have insisted that eschatology is the supreme doctrine—it sums up all of the others and brings them to their fulfillment."[1] All theologies are aimed at fulfilling God's ultimate goal. In this manner, it has been maintained that the whole of theology is eschatology, and thus, eschatology is the sum of theology.

Admittedly, isn't the need for security in the afterlife the greatest motivator of our present frail human existence? Wouldn't it help us to live out our daily lives better if we had an idea of what the future holds, even if in only general terms? Despite our present difficulties and pains, we could live by faith in God's promises regarding our future resurrection knowing that this life is only temporary, and we could set our joy before us as we await to be with our Savior forever in a beautiful and awesome new world. God is certainly excited about our future together! Shouldn't we? Faith and certainty in God's wonderful plan would change our total perspective on life, and our attention could be placed on our actual responsibility during these present days.

---

[1] Millard J. Erickson, *Christian Theology*, 2nd ed. (Grand Rapids, MI: Baker Academic, 1998), 1157.

Yet, what if we have placed our hope on a flawed picture of the future? What if the expectations that we hold are never going to materialize, and the reality that we see unfolding does not fit our preconceived notions? Many have claimed that they know the answers to the eschatological riddle, but at least they tried to understand it. Sadly, too many ignore the apocalyptic texts in the Bible, or accept at face value what others teach about them without more investigation and analysis.

But a correct understanding of eschatology is very important to God's people if we are to recognize and rejoice in what He is doing in our midst. Since we are believers and children of the light, His coming should not take us by surprise, and we can focus our prayers and activities towards God's end plan, preparing ourselves for whatever difficulties or situations that may lie ahead while living a life that is pleasing to Him in the present.

My personal calling, as I understand it, is to present the results of my investigation primarily to the Christian world, but I would also be thrilled if some Jews were to read it, hoping and praying that perhaps some may seriously consider the principles laid out here. I understand that it is essential that we begin this study with a solid Biblical foundation that supports a correct eschatology so as to reach an end-time theology more closely according to God's eternal truths and purposes with mankind. Even if I may be wrong in some interpretations, as it is totally possible, I pray that my basic fundamental premises be as solid as they can be. Hopefully, it may also serve as a warning to unbelievers about their closing window of redemption, so that they may believe in Jesus as the promised Messiah and coming King, and be included in this once-in-a-lifetime event.

The Bible translation more often used for Biblical references in this book is the English Standard Version (ESV), unless otherwise indicated.

Brief Eschatological History of the Church

Most of the early Church, until the early 4th century, believed in the coming of the Lord Jesus to raise His people **after** the tribulation, not before, in accordance with the teachings of Jesus, Paul, and John. This is reflected in the last part of the *Didaché*, which simply means "teachings," also titled *"The Lord's Teaching through the Twelve Apostles to the Nations."* This is a fundamental description of the belief system of the generations following Jesus' ascension, probably written near the end of the 1st century. Regarding the coming of the Lord, it says:

> "(16:3) For **in the last days** false prophets and corrupters shall be multiplied, and the sheep shall be turned into wolves, and love shall be turned into hate; (16:4) for when **lawlessness increases**, they shall hate and persecute and betray one another, and then shall appear the **world-deceiver as Son of God**, and shall do signs and wonders, and the earth shall be delivered into his hands, and he shall do iniquitous things which have never yet come to pass since the

beginning. (16:5) Then shall the creation of men come into the **fire of trial**, and many shall be made to stumble and shall perish; but **those who endure in their faith shall be saved from under the curse itself**. (16:6) And then shall appear the signs of the truth: first, the sign of an **outspreading in heaven**, then the **sign of the sound of the trumpet**. And third, **the resurrection of the dead** (16:7) -- yet not of all, but as it is said: 'The Lord shall come and all **His saints** with Him.' (16:8) Then shall the world see the Lord coming upon the clouds of heaven" (emphases added by this author).[2]

Clearly, this sums up the common early Christian eschatological position that there would be a time when false teachers and general lawlessness would appear, including a "world-deceiver" or Antichrist, who would do evil things as have never been done before, even calling himself son of God. This would represent a time of great "fire of trial" (or tribulation) on earth, and people would stumble and perish, but those Christians who persevered would be "saved from under the curse itself" (*Didaché* 16:5), according to the translation by Roberts-Donaldson. **Then** will the **signs** appear in heaven along with the trumpet sound, and the Lord will raise His saints. Afterwards, the world will see Him coming back upon the clouds of heaven. Regarding the enigmatic phrase of "saved from under the curse itself," some think that the "curse" is a possible reference to Galatians 3:13 (and Deut. 21:22-23), which says that Jesus was made a

---

[2] *Didache*, *Early Christian Writings*, chap. 16, trans. Roberts-Donaldson, http://www.earlychristian writings.com/text/didache-roberts.html (accessed August 21, 2018).

curse for us. That is why J.B. Lightfoot and Kirsopp Lake translated this phrase: "saved by the curse Himself" (Lightfoot) or "saved by the curse itself" (Lake). Charles H. Hoole translated it as "saved by the rock of offence."[3] On the other hand, some believe that it refers to the curse of the Antichrist, under which everyone will come, as understood by Wieland Willker from Greek/English interlinear translation, edition Funk/Bihlmeyer (1924)[4], where the phrase was rendered as "saved above the curse." The Greek preposition in the text is υπ" (including the mark),[5] which is only part of both "under" or "over" in Greek. When these are used in their full form, the Greek words could be *upó* (under) or *upér* (over), which is why we see different and apparently contradictory translations.

Kittel and Friedrich's Greek commentary explains that *upér* could also give a meaning of **protection or defense**,[6] as in Mark 9:40, which says: *"For the one who is not against us is for* [upér] *us."* This example describes how Jesus is above us and intervenes for us; He works on our behalf and in our defense. This idea makes better sense in the referred sentence of the *Didaché*. Neither "saved over" or "saved under" quite explain the meaning as well as "protected." Thus, it could mean: "…those who endure in their faith shall be protected through the Antichrist's curse itself." This interpretation would show

---

[3] *Didache*, four different translations in *Early Christian Writings*, chap. 16, http://www.earlychristian writings.com/didache.html (accessed August 21, 2018).

[4] *Didache*, interlinear Greek-English version by Facsimiliter, http:// facsimiliter.com/Documents/ DidacheIlnr.htm (accessed August 21, 2018).

[5] *Didache*, interlinear Greek-English version by Psalm 119 Foundation, https://www.psalm11918.org /References/Apocrypha/The-Interlinear-Didache.html (accessed August 21, 2018).

[6] Gerhard Kittel and Gerhard Friedrich, eds. *Theological Dictionary of the New Testament*, Vol. VIII, trans. Geoffrey W. Bromiley (Grand Rapids, MI: Eerdmans, 1968), 508.

that early Christians believed that we will experience the time of tribulation or "fire of trial," but will be protected by Jesus Himself in the midst of it, something like we see in Revelation 12:13-17, where the woman (Israel) was *"nourished for a times, and times, and half a time"* while in the wilderness (Rev. 12:14).

This paragraph also clearly states that the "world-deceiver" will have already been revealed, and the earth will have been delivered into his hands, before the resurrection. The last part of this section of the *Didaché* says that "**then**" there will appear signs in heaven, the sound of a trumpet, followed by the resurrection of the dead, but only of the saints, since the unbelievers would not be raised until later. After that, it simply adds that the saints would *"come with"* the Lord when He returns in the clouds, clearly referring to Christ's second coming to establish His kingdom. This phrase is based on Jesus' description of the cataclysmic signs in Matthew 24, after which He would appear to gather His saints.

It is very important to note that Matthew 24 only mentions Jesus **appearing in the clouds** to gather His elect, not really "coming," which is why this cannot count as His "second coming." That will happen at a later moment, when He returns to earth with His saints to put down all rebellion and set up His Kingdom, as in Revelation 19:14, 1 Corinthians 15:22-24 and Jude 1:14. Those last sentences in the *Didaché* clearly contradict the idea that the resurrection and the second coming are the same event, because it separates them into two distinct moments. That is one of the elements of the Postribulationist view that I disagree with, preferring the common **Pretribulationist** notion of two separate events.

On the other hand, even though the *Didaché* pictures the Antichrist as already being revealed to the world and demonstrating his powers and deceit before the resurrection of the saints actually occurs, this does not quite correlate with what Paul described in 2 Thessalonians 2:1-12. This topic will be discussed later, but here we must decide whether we will place the *Didaché* above the Biblical Scripture, or place Scripture above the *Didaché*. I will always place the Biblical and inspired text above any other human writing, including that of early Christians. It is possible that, since this was written by Christians of the 1st century who had already seen the destruction of the Temple and Jerusalem, they were interpreting that the Roman Empire was the embodiment of the Man of Lawlessness and placed his dominion as occurring before the resurrection, rather than after it.

Similarly, when we study Christian writings of the 2nd century, like those by Justin, Tertullian, Lactantius, and Hippolytus, we can find this same strong belief that they were already seeing the Great Tribulation, as many believers were being persecuted and many killed for their faith in Christ.[7] Their hope was that this suffering would finally end with their resurrection, the judgment of the unbelievers, and the establishment of the Messianic Kingdom, **Postribulational** perspective that I share. It is also possible to deduce that they distinguished between the Tribulation and the later Wrath of God against the nations, which is one of the **Midtribulational** ideas that I concur with. Yet I defend the **Pretribulational** idea that the Antichrist's government will not be fully revealed until after the resurrection of the saints. Definitely, with our advantage of hindsight, it was not Rome. But this requires analyzing what is really meant by "Great Tribulation" and distinguishing it from "normal tribulations" that Christians must suffer. This will also be discussed later.

With the passing of time, other eschatological ideas were proposed by Christian leaders and scholars, influenced by the socio-political climate of their days, the growth of anti-biblical Gnosticism and the

---

[7] Erickson, *A Basic Guide to Eschatology*, 149-150.

excessive use of allegory. By the early 4th century, as things seemed more favorable to the Church, thanks to the freedom and prosperity brought by Constantine's Roman Empire in AD 313, there was also less interest in a future resurrection and Messianic Kingdom, and a stronger belief in a Millennium that had allegedly already arrived through the Christianization of the world. Some considered that Christ's second coming would be after the Millennium, which they were allegedly experiencing at the moment, thus giving rise to **Postmillennialism**.

According to the historian Brian E. Daley,[8] Origen of Alexandria, an ascetic and controversial theological author of the early 3rd century, already tended to spiritualize the Kingdom of God and described it as the Church itself, "the assembly of the firstborn and of the unspotted members of the Church that has no blemish," thus defending **Amillennialism**. In his chapter regarding the consummation of the world (in *De Principiis* 3.6.6,) he stressed that "this should not be understood to happen suddenly, but gradually and by steps, as the endless and enormous ages slip by, and the process of improvements and correction advances by degrees in different individuals."[9] He also preferred the concept of immortality of the soul over a literal physical resurrection, the latter which to him reflected "impoverished thoughts."[10]

Eusebius, of the 4th century, imitated Origen's example of spiritualizing eschatology and was even contemptuous of previous apocalyptic ideas. He believed in a "realized eschatology," an

---

[8] Brian E. Daley, *The Hope of the Early Church: A Handbook of Patristic Eschatology* (Grand Rapids, MI: Baker Academic, 1991) 49.

[9] Ibid.

[10] Ibid, 53.

already established Kingdom on earth through the Church.[11] Gregory of Nyssa proposed that the resurrection was nothing but a restoration of the soul from its fallen nature into its ideal form.[12] Augustine of Hippo was also of the Amillennial school, interpreting that the thousand years began with Christ's earthly life and would continue to the end of the church age.[13] Millennialism was even condemned as a superstition at the Council of Ephesus in the year 431.

Later, during the Middle Ages, many Church Protestants and reformers interpreted the book of Revelation as a symbolic historical outline of past church history but with a **Premillennialist** view of Jesus' return, and identified the Pope as the Antichrist, rather than the Roman emperor.[14] This historicist interpretation was identified as the "Protestant" perspective in contrast to the Catholic Church's most common Postmillennialist and/or Amillennialist stance, usually minimizing the importance of the return of Christ. Martin Luther focused on this Premillennialist interpretation, while John Calvin was more cautious, possibly because of the excesses of some Anabaptists in 1534. But by the end of the 18th century European Enlightenment, Postmillennialism again became the dominant view in conservative churches, such as that preached by Daniel Whitby (1638-1726), whose eschatological perspective gained much influence. He believed that the world would first be converted to Christ, the Jews would be restored to their land, and the Pope and the Turks (who still dominated the Holy Land at the time) would ultimately

---

[11] Daley, 77.

[12] Ibid, 87.

[13] George Eldon Ladd, *The Blessed Hope: A Biblical Study of the Second Advent and the Rapture* (Grand Rapids: Eerdmans, 1956), 31.

[14] Ibid, 32.

be defeated. The earth would enjoy a time of universal peace for a thousand years and then Christ would return for the last judgment.[15] None yet held a purely futuristic view of the Tribulation and the Antichrist.

---

[15] Robert G. Clouse, ed., *The Meaning of the Millennium* (Downers Grove, IL: InterVarsity Christian Fellowship, 1977), 11.

3

Quick Summary of Main Premillennial Theories

Before I begin to lay out my thoughts about how the eschatological pieces of the puzzle seem to fit together more cohesively, I must clarify some of the basic propositions of the three main Premillennial theories, namely the Pre-, Mid-, and Post- Tribulational "rapture" ideas. I will list a few of the thoughts that each represent, and then I will proceed to defend my own theory, which contains some elements of each of these, but is very different to all three.

a. Pretribulational "Rapture"

In general, here is a short list of the main Pretribulational basic doctrines:

1. The "rapture of the Church" is to be before a future literal seven-year period of Tribulation.
2. Israel will not be included in the "rapture" because the Jews won't believe in the Messiah until after the Tribulation has begun, or perhaps not until the Millennium.

3. The "elect" in Matthew 24 refers only to the Jews, who will experience the Great Tribulation, but not the Church.

4. The Christian "rapture" will be secret and silent.

5. Since no more prophetic events need to take place, it could be imminent.

6. The "Lawless one," or Antichrist, will be revealed after the "restrainer" is taken out of the way, referring to the Holy Spirit and the Church.

7. God will take His Church before the "Tribulation" because He doesn't want them to endure His wrath.

8. Since the word "church" is not used in Revelation after 4:1, the saints that are mentioned later only refer to people who will accept Christ through a spiritual revival during the "Tribulation," and many will be saved.

9. Some propose that there will be several types of resurrections for different kinds of people, including a later resurrection for those converted during the "Tribulation."

10. The marriage supper of the Lamb will happen in heaven during the "Tribulation," after which time the Lord will come to earth with His Bride.

11. Some propose that the Church is the only "Bride" of Christ. Old Testament saints are just "friends" or "guests" of the groom.

12. The "day of the Lord" is the seven-year period that begins with the rapture of the Church, and includes the Tribulation, the Bowls of Wrath, and the return of Christ to establish His Kingdom.

13. The "rapture" closes the dispensation of the Church, and everything returns to the dispensation of the Law for a completion of Daniel's 70th week.

Some Pretribulationists may have different ways of interpreting these and other aspects, but this is the general consensus among them. We will notice a repetition of some of the same elements in the Mid- and Post- Tribulational theories, while other elements may be different, be contrary, or even new.

b. Midtribulational "Rapture"

Here is a short list of the main Midtribulational basic doctrines:

1. The "rapture" of the Church will occur in the middle of the literal seven-year period of "Tribulation." There are arguments whether it will be after the Sixth Seal or right before the Bowls of Wrath, depending on what they understand as the "Day of the Lord."
2. Israel will not be included in the "rapture" because they won't believe in the Messiah until the second half of the "Tribulation."
3. The "elect" in Matthew 24 refers to Christians, who will experience the first 3½ years of "Tribulation."
4. The "rapture" will be not be secret or silent.
5. The cosmic disturbances of Matthew 24:29 and Joel 2:31 will precede the "rapture" and trigger the Day of the Lord.
6. The "Lawless one," or Antichrist, will be revealed during the first half of the "Great Tribulation" before the "restrainer" is taken out of the way, referring to the Holy Spirit and the Church.
7. God will take His Church because He doesn't want them to endure His "Bowls of Wrath" during the second half of the "Tribulation."

8. The saints that are mentioned after Revelation 4 refer to all the Christians who will be going through the first half of the "Tribulation," and many will be saved.

9. Some believe that there will be an interval between when Christ comes for His saints and later comes with His saints (as in Pretribulationism), while others allege that there is only one *Parousia*, which includes the "rapture" of the Church, the outpouring of God's wrath, and Christ's physical return in glory as a simultaneous event.[16]

10. There is only one resurrection for the saints and then one for the unbelievers at the end of the Millennium.

11. The "Day of the Lord," or end of the age, refers to the whole transition period between the "rapture" in the middle of the "Tribulation" up to the Millennium, but does not include the Millennium.

c. Postribulational "Rapture"

Here is a short list of the main Postribulational doctrines, with a few variants:

1. The "Tribulation" is already being experienced since the beginning of Church history (Payne and Reese), or there is an additional future period of "Great" Tribulation (Gundry), or it has not yet come because it will be a future literal seven-year period of Tribulation (Ladd), after which will be the rapture/ resurrection of the Church.

---

[16] Rosenthal, 221-222.

2. It is generally recognized that Israel will sooner or later be saved, though there are differences as to whether Israel will be saved during the "Day of the Lord" and Tribulation, or during the Millennium.
3. The "elect" in Matthew 24 refers to both Christians and Jews who will experience the "Tribulation," after which Jesus will appear to gather His elect.
4. Some believe that there will be an interval between when Christ comes *for* His saints, and later comes *with* His saints (as in Pre- and Mid- Tribulationism), and others allege that there is only one *Parousia*, which includes the "rapture" of the Church, the outpouring of God's wrath, and Christ's physical return in glory without any intermediate phase.
5. The "rapture" will not be secret or silent.
6. God will protect His people during the first 3½ years of "Great Tribulation" before He raises them up.
7. Some agree that the "Lawless one," or Antichrist, will be revealed before the resurrection (not really understanding what the "restrainer" actually refers to), and some believe that he won't be revealed until after.
8. The saints that are mentioned following Revelation 4 refer to all the Christians (Jews and Gentiles) who experience the "Tribulation" and are saved.
9. The cosmic disturbances of Matthew 24:29 and Joel 2:31 will precede the "rapture," which will trigger the "Day of the Lord" and the Bowls of Wrath.

10. There is only one resurrection for the saints and then one for the unbelievers at the end of the Millennium.

11. There is no ending to an alleged "Church age" and restoration of the "Jewish age." We will all be together in the same Messianic Age.

4

Contentions with the Pretribulational Rapture Theory

Because the Pretribulational Rapture theory is presently the most widely accepted version of all the main eschatological theories, I will only address below the contentions that I have with this one. This theory presents very big problems that I hope will lead many to question the credibility of this theory, because that is all it is. It is only one theory among many, and Christians should be allowed to debate it publically in order to create more awareness of its dubious foundation and to analyze other propositions. I pray that my own theory, which I will later propose, may be more convincing than this one, or that at least it might trigger more debate and study.

a. Questioning its origins

The theory of "dispensationalism" and its resultant popular eschatological position known as "Pretribulational rapture" is being taught from many pulpits as if it were an undisputable doctrine. A great number of Christians these days have accepted this recent theological theory mainly because either they don't have a convincing alternative, they think they don't have the time or ability to find another one, or they feel they don't have the right to question their pastors and teachers, who must know better than they. It seems like they undervalue the role of the Holy Spirit and their personal investigative capacity to seek out Biblical truth on their own. If they at least searched its source, they could see how it could be accused of dubious origins and would question its totally extra-biblical foundation.

John Nelson Darby (1800-1882) was one of several Bible teachers in Ireland, Scotland, and England who were greatly impacted by the preaching of Edward Irving and his futuristic premillennial view around 1830. Darby originally belonged to the Church of England, then became a leader in the Plymouth Brethren movement, and later formed a strict group of churches known as the Exclusive Brethren (also called "Darbyites"). Samuel Prideaux Tregelles,[17] one of the main leaders of Darby's movement who later opposed him, claimed that Darby's Pretribulationist theology was based on an "utterance" of a young lady named Margaret MacDonald from Edward Irving's church in Scotland who allegedly had a "special insight" into the second coming of Christ and which was accepted as "the voice of the Spirit."[18] Tregelles wrote: "…it was from that supposed revelation that the modern doctrine and the modern phraseology respecting it arose. It came not from Holy Scripture, but from that which falsely

---

[17] A well-respected scholar whose published works include *The Englishman's Greek Concordance*, *The Englishman's Hebrew and Chaldee Concordance*, and an English translation of *Gesenius' Hebrew and Chaldee Lexicon to the Old Testament*.

[18] Robert G. Clouse, "Rapture of the Church" in *Evangelical Dictionary of Theology*, edited by Walter A. Elwell, 2nd ed. (Grand Rapids, MI: Baker Academic, 2001), 983-985.

pretended to be the Spirit of God..."[19] Nevertheless, a careful reading of MacDonald's text seems more like a Postribulational defense rather than a Pretribulational one, given phrases like: "The trial of the Church is from Antichrist. It is by being filled with the Spirit that we shall be kept."[20] It is now in doubt whether Darby was actually influenced by this "utterance."

On the other hand, Gundry relates that in 1832, a follower of Irving named Robert Baxter described a "revelation" he had about Jesus' return to be occurring in 1,260 days from that day:[21] the saints would be raptured to heaven, the Antichrist would reign, and then Jesus would return with His saints, according to Irving's previous teachings. Irving was finally excommunicated from the Church of Scotland in 1833, but his theory was further elaborated and promoted by Darby. It was popularized worldwide by means of many prophetic conferences over several years in the United States and Canada.

Darby also developed what is called "Dispensationalism," or the division of Biblical periods into supposedly distinct "dispensations," namely: Paradise, Noah, Abraham, Israel, Gentiles, the Spirit, and the Millennium.[22] These "dispensations" or time segments allegedly

---

[19] Samuel Prideaux Tregelles, *The Hope of Christ's Second Coming* (6th ed., with appendix by C. Y. Biss), England: Witstable Litho, 1886), 22, https://rediscoveringthebible.com/Tregelles1.pdf (accessed January 22, 2019).

[20] *The Preterist Archive*, excerpted from "The Incredible Cover-up" by Dave MacPherson (1975), 171-176. https://www.preteristarchive.com/dEmEnTiA/1975_macpherson_incredible-coverup.html (accessed 3/13/19).

[21] In "Narrative of Facts Characterizing the Supernatural Manifestations in Members of Mr. Irving's Congregation..." cited by Gundry, *The Church and the Tribulation,* 185-186.

[22] Later Pretribulationists, such as Scofield, have their own set of "dispensations," and the newer "progressive dispensationalists" also have a different set of time periods.

describe the way God has treated Israel and all of humankind throughout history, each one independent of the other. Fundamental to his teaching was the absolute separation of Israel and the Church into two distinct peoples of God, and that these have no present or future connection to each other.

Because of him, most Christians have generally termed the Old Testament period after Moses as the "Dispensation of the Law" and the present New Testament Church period as the "Dispensation of Grace," which is actually a fallacy since the Law has never been totally absolved, and Grace was always an essential part of God's Law. But Darby claimed that Israel, and even the Gospels, are part of the old dispensation that was done away with at the cross, and that from then on we have been living in the "age of Grace," unrelated to the Law in any way. Even Nathaniel West opposed this unscriptural position in 1893, saying that "Pretribulationists removed the Olivet Discourse from the church, and the church from the Tribulation."[23]

Cyrus I. Scofield supported Darby's propositions and produced a Bible with personal commentaries from beginning to end, giving the impression that they were just as inspired as the Biblical text. He defined a "dispensation" in his note on Genesis 1:27 as "a period of time during which man is tested in respect of obedience to some specific revelation of the Will of God. Seven such dispensations are distinguished in Scripture."[24] But the apostle Paul referred to a dispensation as God's call or plan regarding Christian stewardship for the dispensing of the Gospel until the fullness of time (1 Cor.

---

[23] Richard R. Reiter, "A History of the Development of the Rapture Positions" in *Three Views on the Rapture: Pre-, Mid-, or Post-Tribulation*, Stanley N. Gundry, series editor, and Gleason L. Archer, general editor (Grand Rapids, MI: Zondervan, 1996), 16-17.

[24] *The Holy Bible*, Rev. C. I. Scofield, ed. (NY: Oxford University Press, 1945), 5.

9:17; Eph. 1:10), a totally different understanding of the term. The Greek word *oikonomia* can be translated literally as the administration or management of a household, since it comes from *oikos*, which means "house," and *nomia*, which means "law or rule." In Paul's letters, it usually means a calling from God for the administration of salvation. The King James Version (KJV) translates the word in 1 Corinthians 9:17 as a *"dispensation of the gospel is committed to me,"* while the English Standard Version (ESV) translates it as being *"entrusted with a stewardship."* In Ephesians 1:10, the KJV translates *oikonomia* as the *"dispensation of the fullness of times,"* while the ESV translates is as *"a plan for the fullness of times."* It simply means that Christians are called to administer the way of salvation to all the world in order to fulfill God's ultimate plans and purposes.

An important fact is that the Pretribulational theory was never part of the Church's theology or eschatology until Darby promoted it. Referring to the recent appearance of this theory in the history of the Church, the well-respected Postribulational theologian George E. Ladd said: "Every Church father who deals with the subject expects the Church to suffer at the hands of Antichrist…The prevailing view is a posttribulation premillennialism. We can find no trace of pretribulationism in the early church; and no modern pretribulationist has successfully proved that this particular doctrine was held by any of the church fathers or students of the Word before the nineteenth century."[25] Not only is it of recent appearance, but Ladd states that this doctrine has not even been able to prove its credibility because it is based on non-Biblical assumptions.

Even the theologian Millard J. Erickson, after comparing Pre- with Post- Tribulationism, concludes that "the balance of evidence

---

[25] Ladd, *The Blessed Hope*, 31.

favors postribulationism."[26] Sadly enough, as Erickson says, most conservative theologians and preachers nowadays do not dare contradict these respected conservative teachers because they don't have a convincing alternative. "Many lay persons, having heard no other view presented, have come to think of dispensationalism as the only legitimate approach to eschatology."[27] This was especially accentuated by fictional novels like Hal Lindsey's *Late Great Planet Earth* in 1971 and Tim LaHaye's novels and movies of *Left Behind*. When people still read these novels and see these movies, they interpret these imaginative theories as though they are pure Biblical doctrine.

b. Questioning its hermeneutics

Pretribulationists basically ignore two hermeneutical principles, which are, firstly, that apocalyptic Biblical figures and numbers are usually symbolic in nature, and secondly, that many prophetic references can already be in our past. But if we portend that everything is literal (as upheld by the literalists) and that they all refer to the future (as upheld by the futurists), we can skew the whole final picture.

Regarding the literalist tendency, Erickson highlights this as especially problematic about Darby's eschatological perspective. He used strict literal hermeneutics when the text was intended to be metaphorical, but metaphorical when it was supposed to be literal.[28] He interpreted some of the Bible's intended apocalyptic symbolism to a literal level of absurdity, but ignored its important literal message

---

[26] Erickson, *Christian Theology*, 1231.

[27] Ibid, 1159.

[28] Millard J. Erickson, *A Basic Guide to Eschatology: Making Sense of the Millennium* (Grand Rapids, MI, Baker Books, 1998), 109.

regarding the Church's relation to Israel. These hermeneutics have been taken to an extreme where nothing makes Scriptural sense, yet fundamental Pretribulationists defend it as the only correct way of interpretation. Sadly, people can make the Scriptures say whatever they want. But we must follow some general rules of Biblical interpretation so that we are not blinded by our own prejudices or presumptions (to be discussed later).

Regarding the futurist versus historicist issue, we should look at history in an honest way to see whether some things have already been fulfilled or not, and what things still lie in our future. Some events were meant to occur in the future of the prophet, but are now found in our own past. Not all that was in the prophet's future is still in our own future. Though some Bible teachers claim that prophecies can have a double fulfillment, once in the general time of the prophet and then again in latter days, we should be very cautious with this, because it can confuse the facts and skew the intended interpretation of the prophecy.

The modern conflict that exists between the Pre-, Mid-, and Post-Tribulational theories is mostly centered on two Bible texts. The first one is 1 Thessalonians 4:17, and the second one is Daniel 9:24-27. The way that these are interpreted gives basis for interpreting other texts in order to match it. These are the two main points of departure for the various end-time theories.

We will first look at the text from Paul's letter to the Thessalonians, and then later on we will discuss the text in Daniel 9.

> *"Then we who are alive, who are left, will be **caught up** together with them in the clouds to meet the Lord in the air, and so we will always be with the Lord"* (1 Thess. 4:17).

There is nothing here that indicates a specific timing of when this being "caught up" will occur, but the modern term "rapture" itself, obtained from this text, carries a lot of baggage and presumes a whole set of conclusions. This term just describes **how** Jesus will raise the living believers when He returns to gather His people. The original Greek verb for "caught up" is *harpazo*, while the Latin verb is "*raptare*," which has been converted to a noun, thus calling it a "rapture." But the verb simply describes the theological term known as "resurrection from the dead."

It is essential, at this point, to discuss the confusion that lies behind the unique "rapture" terminology. Pretribulationism differentiates between "rapture" and "resurrection" as though they were different events. The correct and Biblical term has always been "resurrection," since this is the noun, and being "caught up" is merely a verb, one of the visible manifestations at the moment of the resurrection (whether of the still living or of the dead). It can also be described as a "rising up," as in the Hebrew word "*kum*" of Isaiah 26:19, and also as a "gathering" or "assembling together" of God's people, as in the Greek term "*episunogage*" of 2 Thessalonians 2:1. Some people also claim that the term "resurrection" only applies to those who will be actually dead, while "rapture" refers to those who will still be alive when Jesus raises them up. This distinction is quite unnecessary, since "resurrection" refers to both the dead and those that are still living at the time of the resurrection. Alexander Reese, in 1937, clarified the following regarding the terminology of resurrection versus rapture: "…we may dismiss the Rapture from our minds, and confine our attention to the first resurrection, for wheresoever the resurrection is, there will the Rapture be also."[29]

---

[29] Alexander Reese, *The Approaching Advent of Christ* (Grand Rapids, MI: International Publications Edition: 1975 reprint), 34.

Sadly, this idea of being "caught up" leads to a position that only the Church will be "raptured" while Israel stays behind for the "Tribulation." This theory seems to willfully discard, ignore or misinterpret Jesus' own words from His Olivet Discourse about **when** He would gather "His elect":

> *"Immediately **after** the tribulation of those days the sun will be darkened, and the moon will not give its light, and the stars will fall from heaven, and the powers of the heavens will be shaken. **Then** will appear in heaven the sign of the Son of Man, and **then** all the tribes of the earth will mourn, and they will see the Son of Man coming on the clouds of heaven with power and great glory. And he will send out his angels with a loud trumpet call, and they will **gather his elect** from the four winds, from one end of heaven to the other"* (Matt. 24:29-31; similar to Mk. 13:3-27).

The Pretribulational "rapture" theory alleges that this reference of Jesus appearing to "gather His elect" **after** the "Tribulation" only refers to Israel and the Jewish people, not to the Church. But if we look objectively at the context in Matthew (and the parallel passages in Mark and Luke), there is no indication that Jesus was referring only to Israel. He previously mentioned worldwide wars, natural disasters, and increased lawlessness, as well as persecution against Christians while they proclaim the Gospel to all nations. There is also a reference to the abomination on the Temple Mount and that Jerusalem would be trampled *"until the times of the Gentiles is fulfilled"* (Lk. 21:24), which is when He used the term of "great tribulation." Here is where we must be honest with the text, and notice that Jesus was referring to something that evidently occurred in AD 70. In this sense, I agree that Jesus was referring to the Jewish people regarding the "Great Tribulation," but clearly not as something in the future, rather as something already in our past! This totally disrupts the whole Pretribulationist concept of a future Great Tribulation together with the Antichrist! The puzzle pieces of the past "Great Tribulation" are actually **not** going to fit next to the pieces of the future Antichrist, but rather with the extended tribulations suffered by the Jews ever since the 1st century to the modern era! (This will be discussed in more detail later.)

On the other hand, Jesus also said there would be so many false Christs that the "elect" could be led astray by their false teachings, referring to Christians, not to Jews. He added: *"And you will be hated by all for my name's sake. But the one who endures to the end will be saved"* (Mk. 13:13). Jesus exhorted His own disciples that they should be on their guard and persevere in the midst of all these tribulations that they would experience until the very end (Matt. 10:22), because He was sending them as sheep among wolves (Matt. 10:16). And then Jesus clarified that **after** certain ***"tribulations of those days,"*** He would gather His elect, and **not before** (Matt. 24:29-31).

Worst of all, some teach that after the Church's "rapture," many people (including the Jews) will be saved during a literal seven-year window of "Tribulation" and can enter the Kingdom of God without actually being raised from the dead. But this is impossible, since Paul clarified that ***"flesh and blood cannot inherit the kingdom of God***, *nor does the perishable inherit the imperishable"* (1 Cor. 15:50).

In all certainty, a resurrected body is required for inheriting the Father's eternal Kingdom. Unless a person experiences the first resurrection, he or she will never be able to enter the Messianic Kingdom nor the new heavens and new earth. So if Israel does not participate together with the Church in this first resurrection, there is no other moment for the Jews to obtain an imperishable body and enter the Father's Kingdom promised to them even before it was promised to the Christians! Once the imperishable saints return to earth with Jesus for the Messianic Kingdom, they will never die again. Though many unbelievers who do not experience the resurrection of the saints will survive the Bowls of Wrath until the establishment of the Messianic Kingdom and exist for its duration, they will never have another opportunity to obtain imperishable bodies. They will be subjects during the Millennial Kingdom, but will again rebel against God once Satan is allowed to entice them as before. If someone is not included in the once-in-a-lifetime resurrection of the saints, Scripture says that the only resurrection remaining will be the second one meant for judging and condemning unbelievers for eternity at the end of the Millennium. *"Blessed and holy is the one who shares in the* **first resurrection***! Over such the* **second death has no power***…"* (Rev. 20:6).

The Pretribulational "rapture" theory also proposes that the "rapture" will be a very secret and surprising event when Christians suddenly disappear, leaving everyone wondering what happened to them. But proper hermeneutics of Matthew 24 dispels the idea of any secrecy to Jesus' glorious appearance for raising His elect, which will be as visible as the lightning that comes from the east and shines as far as the west (Matt. 24:27). Paul added that at the loud blast of the "last trumpet" (1 Cor. 15:52; 1 Thess. 4:16), the Messiah and His archangel will shout their command for His people to rise. All the peoples of the earth will see Him and hear the great raucous and will mourn because they will recognize that they missed their chance to repent and be saved (Matt. 24:30). Revelation 1:7 adds that *"every eye will see Him"* and will wail.

Pretribulationists also allege that the last trumpet in 1 Corinthians 15:52 and the seventh one mentioned in Revelation 11:12-15 are different, that one is for the believers and the other is for Israel. Yet these are one and the same. There is only one event that the Bible is referring to, which is the one and only long-awaited resurrection spoken of by the ancient prophets, meant originally for the Jewish people, but which also includes the Gentiles through their faith in the Jewish Messiah.

Another text wrongly interpreted by Pretribulationists is Luke 21:36.

> *"But stay awake at all times, praying that you may have strength to **escape** all these things that are going to take place, and to stand before the Son of Man"* (Lk. 21:36, ESV).

They use this verse to justify that Christians will escape the "Tribulation." Nevertheless, the reference in verse 34 to "that day" coming suddenly as a trap clearly refers to the coming of the Son of Man with power and glory at His *Parousia* to punish the nations, not to gather His elect:

> *"But watch yourselves lest your hearts be weighed down with dissipation and drunkenness and cares of this life, and **that day** come upon you suddenly like a trap. For it will come upon all who dwell on the face of the whole earth"* (Lk. 2:34-35).

Oftentimes, when the term "that day" is used in an apocalyptic context, it refers to the terrible Day of the Lord, the day of God's vengeful wrath, such as:

> *"But **the day of the Lord** will come like a thief, and then the heavens will pass away with a roar, and the heavenly bodies*

will be burned up and dissolved, and the earth and the works that are done on it will be exposed" (2 Pet. 3:10).[30]

Thus, in Luke 21:36, Jesus was warning drunkards and sinners that they should repent so as to escape their just punishment when He returns for judgment. They should turn their lives over to God and persevere in their faith so as to stand righteously before the Son of Man when He comes first to gather His saints, instead of being destroyed by God's wrath along with the rest of unbelievers when He returns. This has nothing to do with Christians escaping the "Tribulation," but merely sinners escaping God's wrath through repentance and remaining faithful until the resurrection of the saints.

Another verse used by Pretribulationists is 1 Thessalonians 5:9, which states: *"For God has not destined us for **wrath**, but to obtain salvation through our Lord Jesus Christ."* This is definitely correct, but it refers to the future Bowls of Wrath **after** the resurrection of the saints. It is evident in Scripture that the "Seals" and "Trumpets" in Revelation are not the same as the "Bowls of Wrath," which will definitely come only upon unbelievers at the time when Jesus and His people are celebrating their wedding feast in heaven. So it is correct that God's people will escape His Wrath when *"it will come upon all who dwell on the face of the whole earth"* (Lk. 21:35). But this does not refer to a Pretribulational "rapture." Unbelievers will be the only remaining dwellers on earth at that time.

Another frequently cited verse by these proponents is Revelation 3:10, which says: *"Because you have kept my word about patient endurance, I will **keep you from** ['tereo ek'] the **hour of trial** that is coming on the whole world, to try those who dwell on the earth."*

---

[30] See also Isaiah 13:9-11, Joel 2:10-11, Joel 3:14-15, 1 Thessalonians 5:1-4, and Revelation 16:14.

This is actually a message to the specific church of Philadelphia, which suffered a great deal of persecution under Emperor Trajan in AD 98. Even if there might be some analogy to modern Christians, the Greek term *'tereo ek'* in *"I will keep you from the hour of trial..."* merely refers to God's **protection in the midst of adversity**. Jesus used those words with this same meaning in: *"I do not ask that you **take them out** [airo ek] of the world, but that you **keep them from** [tereo ek] the evil one"* (Jn. 17:15). In both verses, *tereo ek* clearly implies a protection and a guarding of God's people in the midst of tribulation, as a fortress encircles its inhabitants and defends them from their enemy. Thus, Pretribulationists have taken these words to the church of Philadelphia out of their context only to prove what they have already convinced themselves to believe.

One final observation regarding the questionable hermeneutics of the "Pretribulation rapture" theory is that it claims that the Church is never mentioned in the book of Revelation after chapter 3. But this ignores the many mentions of the "saints," which clearly refers to God's people, both Jew and Christian. It is similar to Daniel 7:21, which states that the "horn" will make war against the "saints" and prevail against them. Revelation 14:12-13 describes these "saints" with the phrase: *"...those who keep the commandments of God and their faith in Jesus."* These are God's servants who fear His name (Rev. 11:18), sing the song of Moses, and also the song of the Lamb (Rev. 15:3), saints of both the Old Testament and the New Testament together, those who have conquered the beast and its image before the seven bowls of wrath are to be poured out (Rev. 15:2). They will **all** have gone through their times of tribulation, but will be taken out victoriously before God pours out His wrath upon the remaining people on earth.

c. Replacement and/or Dual Covenant theologies

Darby was not the first Christian theologian to propose that the Church has nothing to do with Israel. Many early Church fathers preached that Israel had been replaced by the Church in God's plans, including Church fathers such as Justin, Irenaeus, and Tertullian during the 2nd century.[31] Origen and Cyprian of the 3rd century taught that the Church was now "the true Israel."[32] Eusebius, of the 4th century, taught that "...the special unction amongst the Jews should be totally abolished,"[33] and that "the divine justice overtook the Jews in this way, for their crimes against Christ.[34]"

By the time Constantine declared Christianity as the official religion of Rome, replacement theology was consolidated in Christian thought, ratified at the First Council of Nicaea in AD 325. Later Christian theologians even became aggressive in their attacks, describing the Jews as perverse and accursed forever (Hilary of Poitiers), a brood of vipers (Gregory of Nyssa), serpents and wearing the image of Judas (Jerome), as well as murderers and possessed by the devil (Chrysostom).[35]

Augustine of Hippo, though milder and more respectful in his *Sermon Against the Jews*, taught that the Jews deserve the most severe

---

[31] Justo L. González, *Historia del Cristianismo, Tomo 1*, (Miami, FL: Unilit, 1994), 87-101.

[32] Daniel Gruber. *The Church and the Jews — the Biblical Relationship* (Springfield, MO: General Council of Assemblies of God Intercultural Ministries, 1991), 11.

[33] Eusebius, *The Ecclesiastical History*, Book I, Ch. VI, 31, trans. Christian Frederick Crusé, Internet Archive (New York: Thomas N. Stanford, 1856), https://archive.org/details/ecclesiasticalhi00euse/page/n8 (accessed August 17, 2018).

[34] Ibid, Book II, Ch. VII, 57.

[35] Clarence H. Wagner, Jr., *Lessons from the Land of the Bible* (Jerusalem, Israel: Faith Publishing, 1998), 146, http://www.ldolphin.org/replacement/ (accessed August 19, 2018).

punishment for having put Jesus to death, but they have been kept alive by Divine Providence to serve, together with their Scriptures, as witnesses to the truth of Christianity. He compared Israel with Esau and the Church with Jacob, where the older served the younger:

> "…are we to deny that the Apostles and those Churches of Judaea… belong to the house of Jacob; or is another people to be understood as the spiritual Jacob other than the Christian people themselves, who, although younger than the people of Judaea, have surpassed them in increases and have replaced them, that the Scripture might be fulfilled in the figure of the two brothers, 'and the elder shall serve the younger'? Sion, however, and Jerusalem, although spiritually understood as the Church, are nevertheless a fitting witness against the Jews."[36]

In this sense, Darby was just following the anti-Semitism that had been taught by countless respected theologians since the 2nd century on, but he changed their eschatological historicism to futurism, and their Posttribulationism to Pretribulationism. This erroneous anti-Semitic view has created such havoc in Christian eschatology that believers don't even understand their true intended relationship with Israel, nor can they envision a spiritual unity between the two, clearly described by Paul in Ephesians chapter 2. Though some Christians interpret this "new man" as referring only to Christians, Paul clearly stated that he meant an actual melding of both Jewish and Gentile believers, creating *"one new man in place of the two…"* (Eph. 2:15),

---

[36] *Augustine's "Treatise against the Jews,"* Ch. 10, posted by Roger Pearse. https://www.roger-pearse.com/weblog/2015/06/11/augustines-treatise-against-the-jews/comment-page-1/ (accessed August 19, 2018).

which is the real purpose of the New Covenant in the Messiah and the fulfillment of all God's plans since the creation of mankind. Christians are not the main purpose of God's salvific plan. We merely have the privilege of being grafted into the olive tree together with Israel (Rom. 11) through the door of faith that was opened to the Gentiles (Acts 14:27) by Jesus' atoning death for all mankind.

Yet the Church after the 4th century often visualized itself as becoming a world-dominating power after spreading the Gospel to every nation, triumphantly equating the Church with Christ's realized Kingdom. In this wrongful reading of Scripture, they said that Israel had been replaced by the Church and that God had no more purpose for Israel and the Jewish people, which is clearly **Replacement Theology**. It was also erroneously argued that the God of the Church is not the same as the God of Israel. Some dispensationalists today even allege that in the end-time days, Jewish believers will inherit the earth and continue to live under the Law, while Christians will inherit heaven and continue to live under Grace. This is an attitude that many modern Pretribulationists have inherited from early Church fathers, whether they are aware of it or not. Even though some defenders of Pretribulational theory might say that they love Israel and that they are not really anti-Semitic, this negative perspective of Israel permeates Pretribulationism. It teaches that Israel must be left behind to suffer greater tribulation than it has so far, reflecting a pronounced Christian elitism. They believe that only the Church will receive the promise of resurrection, while Israel will see God's judgment. Some even say that Israel will be persecuted in the future "Great Tribulation" so badly that "Hitler will look like a baby."

Actually, the resurrection of the dead is of such central importance in Judaism that it is said it "became with them an article of faith, the denial of which was condemned as sinful."[37] The Mishnah's *Sanhedrin* 10:1 states: "He who says that there is no resurrection of the dead must be counted among those who have no share in the future world." The longest Jewish discussion on the resurrection is in *Sanhedrin* 90a-92a. Their prayer books are also full of references to a hope in the resurrection of the dead, including their daily prayer of *Amidah*, as stated in the Benediction #2:

> "You are eternally mighty, my Lord, the **Resuscitator of the dead** are You; abundantly able to save... He sustains the living with kindness, **resuscitates the dead** with abundant mercy, supports the fallen, heals the sick, releases the confined, and **maintains His faith to those asleep in the dust**. Who is like You, O Master of mighty deeds, and who is comparable to You, O King Who **causes death and restores life** and makes salvation sprout?... And You are faithful to **resuscitate the dead**. Blessed are You, Hashem, who **resuscitates the dead**."[38]

All Jewish prayers and commentaries uphold those Scriptural beliefs, and were also confirmed by two of the greatest Jewish theologians, namely Saadia Gaon Ben Yosef (AD 882-942) and Maimonides (1135-1204). Saadia Gaon reiterated and added to the mainstream Pharisaic beliefs regarding a physical resurrection and is generally regarded as representative of most Orthodox and many Conservative perspectives due to his adherence to earlier Biblical and Pharisaic Judaism. On the other hand, Maimonides' writings

---

[37] Abraham Cohen, *Everyman's Talmud*, (New York: Schocken Books, 1995), 357.

[38] *The Complete Artscroll Siddur, Weekly, Sabbath, Festival* (Nusach Ashkenazi), trans. Rabbi Nosson Scherman, 2nd ed. (New York: Mesorah Publ. Ltd, 1998), 107.

represent a slight departure from traditional Orthodox Judaism, as he introduced a more spiritualized interpretation of resurrection. Nonetheless, he provided an important document that is supported by most orthodox groups, called the *Thirteen Principles of Faith*, which are espoused by all Jews no matter what their tendencies are.

Of exceptional importance is the fact that Maimonides acknowledged in his *Book of Knowledge* that some righteous Gentiles could even be included in the resurrection: *"The pious of the Gentiles will have a share in the World to Come"* (*Hilkhot Teshuvah* 3:5). The Jewish author Abraham Cohen confirms that it is now a "fairly official Jewish doctrine" that there will be righteous men who will participate in the World to Come.[39]

There is also an ancient rabbinic idea that when God revealed Himself and gave the *Torah* on Mount Sinai to His people, He not only gave them the choice between death and life, but they actually experienced death and were brought back to life. According to this *midrash*, the people of Israel died after hearing God's voice from its sheer intensity, and God then raised them from the dead by means of His dew, referring to Isaiah 26:19, which says: *"Your dead shall live; their bodies shall rise. You who dwell in the dust, awake and sing for joy! For your dew is a dew of light, and the earth will give birth to the dead."* According to the Jewish scholar Jon D. Levenson, "God pre-enacts the eschatological resurrection then and there, with the selfsame agent (the dew) with which he will revive the deceased of all generations at the end of days."[40]

Some Pretribulationists might acknowledge and respect this Jewish faith in their own resurrection by stating that God's covenantal

---

[39] Cohen, 369.

[40] Jon D. Levenson, *The Death and Resurrection of Israel: The Ultimate Victory of the God of Life* (New Haven: Yale University, 2006), 226.

promises to Israel will somehow be fulfilled in the long run,[41] but this can sometimes lead to the misplaced belief in a **Dual-Covenant Theology**, where God has separate redemptive methods for each people group. This theology alleges that God will redeem each one in their own way, one by keeping the Law and the other by Grace. But this is in contradiction to John 5:24, which clearly says: *"Jesus said to him, 'I am the way, and the truth, and the life. No one comes to the Father except through me.'"* This means that Israel must believe in Jesus as their Messiah before the resurrection of the righteous occurs, so that God's plans regarding His Jewish people may be fulfilled.

On the other hand, other Pretribulation theologians have invented a "multiple resurrection" theory outside of all Biblical evidence in order to not sound too anti-Semitic. But all these denials of God's promises to Israel regarding their resurrection and Messianic Kingdom reflect not only an anti-Semitic attitude, but is in direct contradiction to all Old and New Testament Scripture. Satan is still trying to keep God's two people groups from becoming one through this incorrect theology, so that God's perfect plan will not be fulfilled.

d. Problems with prophetic timing

In addition to the theological misinterpretations of the Pretribulational rapture theory described above, there is the timing problem that it creates. Pretribulationists allege that God has stopped or paused His eschatological clock, waiting for the moment of the "imminent" rapture, since nothing is lacking in fulfillment for this to happen. This interruption in time is conveniently alleged, without Biblical basis, in order to explain the long time lapse between Jesus' ascension until now. When interpreting the "last week" of Daniel

---

[41] Erickson, *Christian Theology*, 1218.

9:24-27 (which they admit cannot refer to a literal week, yet they reinterpret it as seven years), they say that the eschatological clock has stopped ticking for the past almost 2,000 years, and that Daniel's "last week" is expected to start again with the "rapture" and will continue for the duration of the literal "seven-year tribulation."

Even if the first 69 years in Daniel 9 might have been fulfilled literally regarding the rebuilding of Jerusalem and Jesus' death, as some claim to be able to prove, there is no requirement that the 70th week also be fulfilled literally. We do not need to force the fulfillment of Jesus' words in Matthew 24 into a short seven-year window. It makes more Biblical sense to say that God's grace has been **extended** in order to save more people:

> "But do not overlook this one fact, beloved, that with the Lord **one day is as a thousand years**, and a thousand years as one day. The Lord is not slow to fulfill his promise as some count slowness, but is patient toward you, not wishing that any should perish, but that **all should reach repentance**" (2 Pet. 3:9).

Peter added that we should "count the patience of our Lord as salvation" for the unsaved (v. 15). Furthermore, and most important of all, Jesus said that Jerusalem would not see Him again **until** the Jews say: "Blessed is He who comes in the name of the Lord" (Matt. 23:39). He clearly referred to the desolations of Jerusalem, but also implied that this response is a prerequisite for His coming. We are actually waiting for **this** to be fulfilled before the resurrection of the saints, both Christians and Jews! "O Jerusalem, Jerusalem… I tell you, you will not see me **until you say**, 'Blessed is he who comes in the name of the Lord!'" (Lk. 13:34-35).

At the opening of the Fifth Seal in Revelation, we read that the souls of the martyrs under the heavenly altar cry out: *"…how long before you will judge and avenge our blood on those who dwell on the earth?"* (Rev. 6:9). The answer is that they need to rest a little longer, ***"until the number of their fellow servants and their brothers should be complete, who were to be killed as they themselves had been"*** (Rev. 6:11). Jesus clarified that there would be many wars, *"but **the end will not be at once"*** (Lk. 21:9). This waiting period of about two millennia can also be related to the 400 years that God waited to deliver the Israelites out of Egypt so that the sins of the Egyptian people could reach their utmost, and then God brought judgment upon those who afflicted His people (Gen. 15:13-14).

I believe that Jesus is waiting for the Church to repent and accept its rightful relationship along with Israel. *"Lest you be wise in your own sight, I do not want you to be unaware of this mystery, brothers: a partial hardening has come upon Israel, **until the fullness of the Gentiles has come in"*** (Rom. 11:25). This entire chapter warns Christians against any kind of pride regarding their position alongside Israel, and clearly reflects an **extension** of time while God **waits** for the fullness of the Gentiles to come in. Perhaps God is waiting for both Christians and Jews to drop their prejudices towards each other, and become one body under one Headship.

Yet, this necessitates an explanation for the frequent mention of days or years often used in the apocalyptic passages of Daniel and Revelation, such as 3½ years, 1,260 days, etc. I have no good explanation for them except that those time periods are most probably symbolic and should not be interpreted in a literal manner, considering that this is a characteristic of apocalyptic texts. Even Pretribulationists see the last "week" of Daniel as **partially** symbolic of seven years, but I believe that it should be seen as **totally** symbolic, representing segments of time that are only in God's hand. They seem to be just general extensions of time, depending on mankind's actions or inactions.

God often responds to mankind's repentance or lack of repentance, as in the example of the people of Nineveh. He can also delay the fulfillment of His promises to bless His people, as in the example of God not allowing the first generation of Israelites to enter the Promised Land due to their rebellion, but allowing the second generation to enjoy that privilege because of their more humble and obedient attitude (Num. 32:11-13). God can be longsuffering in His anger, **delaying His punishment**, but also **waiting to show His mercy** in fulfilling His promises, all the while requiring that we also wait for Him in obedience and love. *"Therefore **the LORD waits** to be gracious to you, and therefore he exalts himself to show mercy to you. For the LORD is a God of justice; blessed are all **those who wait for him**"* (Isa. 30:18).

Regarding the interpretation of apocalyptic numbers, Revelation 12 is an example of how numbers are used symbolically to describe general historical events. Israel is the woman giving birth to a male child who is *"is to rule all the nations with a rod of iron, but her child was caught up to God and to his throne"* (verse 5). Satan tried to kill this baby as soon as He was born, and then the woman had to flee to the "wilderness" due to his anger (Israel was exiled from the land of Israel), where she was "nourished" by God *"for 1,260 days"* (verse 6) or *"for a time, and times, and half a time"* (verse 14). History shows that Israel was sustained, yet purified, for an extended period of time until it became a new nation in 1948. Israel's time in exile can also be seen as the same time in which the Church has been persecuted following Jesus' ascension, as described in verse 17:

"Then the dragon became furious with the woman and went off to make war on the rest of her offspring, on those who keep the commandments of God and hold to the testimony of Jesus..."

Thus, we can see the use of a variety of numbers in apocalyptic texts. Daniel 12:11 says that there will be ***"1,290 days"*** between the time when the regular burnt offering is taken away and the abomination that makes desolate is set up. This represents the time between the destruction of the Temple in AD 70 and the construction of the mosque on the Temple Mount in AD 691. That time lapse was certainly not 1,290 literal days, but rather 621 years. There will also supposedly be ***"42 months"*** when this Temple Mount will be trampled upon by the Gentiles (Rev. 11:2), or ***"1,260 days,"*** when God's two witnesses will be prophesying (Rev. 11:3), and who will then be killed by the Beast. The nations will gaze at their deaths for ***"3½ days"*** (Rev. 11:9) before they are taken up by God. Daniel 8:14 also speaks about ***"2,300 evenings and mornings"*** before the sanctuary is restored to its rightful state. This number, if taken literally, makes even less sense than the others, and it possibly refers to a symbolic period of time until the Temple is finally restored in Jerusalem during the time of the Messianic Kingdom. Then there is also a reference to a special blessing for those who wait and arrive at ***"1,335 days"*** (Dan. 12:12).

It is important to note that the above books are of an apocalyptic nature, *'apokalupsis'* meaning "revelation," while apocalyptic eschatology refers to revelation regarding events of the end-times. One of the characteristics of this type of literature, both Biblical and extra-Biblical, is that it uses events, numbers, and people in a purely allegorical form. But as Reddish states, "the [literal] approach taken by Hal Lindsey and others like him is often the only interpretation of apocalyptic literature known to the general public. All interpreters of the canonical books of Daniel and Revelation, including Hal Lindsey, would do well to familiarize themselves with other Jewish and early Christian apocalyptic writings."[42] My position is that there is no literal meaning to these numbers at all, but only a general lapse of time.

---

[42] Mitchell G. Reddish, Ed. *Apocalyptic Literature* (Peabody, Mass.: Hendrickson, 1990), 34-35.

5

Correct Christian and Jewish Hermeneutical Practices

During the process of my analyzing the prophetic passages in the Bible, I was well aware of certain proper hermeneutic practices that I should follow. We must admit that personal preferences or prejudices can cloud the judgment of a believer into thinking that he or she is interpreting Scripture in a good and solid manner. This occurs when we want to prove a point, and so we put our own interpretation *into the text*, which is called **eisegesis**. This person does not extract the meaning *from* the text, but rather imparts his or her own interpretation *to* the text. In contrast, proper hermeneutics is done when the interpreter derives his or her understanding by taking the intended meaning *out of the text* in an honest and objective way, which is called **exegesis**.

The Scripture itself tell us that if anyone intends to properly handle the Word of Truth (2 Tim. 2:15), they must follow a few rules of hermeneutics, or correct methods of Biblical interpretation, so as to avoid, as much as possible, a false conclusion. Peter warned against making personal pronouncements and interpretations, declaring that *"no prophecy of Scripture is a matter of private interpretation"* (2 Pet.

1:20, NASB). Henry A. Virkler proposes that hermeneutics can be a science as well as an art.[43] It is a science when we apply a series of rules in an orderly fashion. It is an art when we add flexibility to the text so that it does not distort the true intention of its meaning, especially in the instance of parables, allegories and prophecies.

A profoundly influential factor when interpreting Bible texts is the way in which a person regards Scripture. One can hold an orthodox view of Scripture, understanding the Bible as God's inspired Word, or a more liberal position, as when the Bible text is perceived as a mere historical document written by human people. Given that I believe that the Bible is a repository of divinely revealed, inerrant, and infallible truth, written by men but directed by God's Spirit, I am challenged by the goal of trying to carefully ascertain what God really meant in a certain passage rather than make it fit a specific agenda or need.

When interpreting Scripture, we will also soon discover other impediments to what should hopefully be a simple understanding of God's text. We can find historical gaps between the time when it was written and our own time, as well as cultural gaps due to differences between our contrasting societies. Furthermore, there are linguistic gaps in the translation of the original texts into our various modern languages, and this is compounded by whether a text may have a simple interpretation and a fuller interpretation (*sensus plenior*), as when a Bible author could have been referring to a situation in his present time and it may also have a fuller meaning in the future, as in prophetic texts. That is why the same message can end up with such contradicting and divergent interpretations.

On the other hand, Scripture is inerrant but can still present

---

[43] Henry A. Virkler, *Hermeneutics: Principles and Processes of Biblical Interpretation* (Grand Rapids, MI: Baker Books, 1999), 16.

some numbers and figures in apparently contradictory ways because often the intention was not to be mathematically precise but to give a general idea, while focusing on more important spiritual principles. That is why numerical reports, as well as eschatological predictions, can be either approximations or symbols. As Virkler declares: "A statement is considered accurate when it meets the level of precision intended by the writer and expected by his audience."[44]

Since the above factors invariably affect our hermeneutics of any given text, we should first objectively determine the original historical-cultural context (not using anti-Biblical historical criticism), then perform a proper lexical-syntactical analysis of the words in their immediate context, and then do a more thorough theological study of similar expressions in the rest of God's Word. Given that much of prophecy can have either a literal or symbolic meaning, or both, we must see how these elements are used in other contexts and make a comparable interpretation of these. Sadly, much distortion can be produced if we interpret something figuratively when it should be seen literally, and literally when it should be seen figuratively. As described by Walvoord, "while there will never be complete agreement on the line between imagery and the literal, the patient exegete must resolve each occurrence in some form of consistent interpretation."[45] Yet I believe that Walvoord's premise that imagery should always be interpreted as literal unless the context offers its symbolic meaning is a **faulty** foundation, since this is probably not a valid rule regarding apocalyptic texts.

We should also always consider the role that God's Holy Spirit desires to play in a proper reading and understanding of His Word. Since even honest Christians can have a selective tendency to

---

[44] Virkler, 44.

[45] John F. Walvoord, *Revelation* (Chicago, Illinois: Moody Publishers, 2011), 29.

see Scripture according to a certain position, we depend on the Holy Spirit to keep us on course so that we can reach a correct understanding of God's communication. Jesus declared that we can only know about future events through the help of the Holy Spirit: *"When the Spirit of truth comes, he will guide you into all the truth, for he will not speak on his own authority, but whatever he hears he will speak, and he will declare to you **the things that are to come***" (Jn. 16:13).

We should also consider the various hermeneutical practices that the Jewish people have used down through history. Ezra the Scribe and the Jerusalem Levites gave a clear, accurate, and literal interpretation of God's Law to the people after returning to the land of Israel from the Babylonian dispersion (Neh. 8:8). This level of interpretation, in modern Jewish terms, is defined as *peshat*, or the simple meaning of a Biblical text.[46] Rabbi Hillel, close to Jesus' time, usually defended this type of interpretation, which is also embodied in the *Mishnah*. Rabbi Ishmael (of the same period) developed a second level of interpreting Scripture, comparing ideas, words, and phrases that are hinted at in more than one text, called *remez*. This was not considered wrongful, yet it led to more imaginative ways of giving meaning not always explicit in the simple text. His thirteen rules of interpretation reflected the type of sometimes fanciful illustrations used in both the Jerusalem and Babylonian *Talmudim*. The *midrash*, or allegorical narration, was used to explain the Biblical text in an ethical or devotional style, though still within a proper understanding of the original intent. Nevertheless, at times it could supersede its intended meaning. During the 2nd century AD, both Jews and Christians began to interpret Scripture in manners dangerously outside of their evident, natural meaning. Christian

---

[46] Philip Birnbaum, *Encyclopedia of Jewish Concepts* (Rockaway Beach, NY: Hebrew Publishing Co, 1991), 331-335.

exegetes tended to allegorize parts of the Scripture in an incorrect and extreme way, eliminating the literal meaning of Israel from the text and substituting it for the "Church." This was done in order to claim God's promises to Israel and remove Israel from the picture. Jewish rabbis also believed that they could give various meanings to a text, especially Rabbi Akiva of the 2nd century, who maintained that every word had hidden ideas, oftentimes carrying it to speculative extremes and deriving an "oral tradition" with just as much authority as God's Word. This practice was taken even further by the mystical *sod* ("secret") interpretations used in the *Sohar*, or "Radiance" of the *Torah*, leading to the use of numerology (a supernatural reading of the numerical value of letters according to their positions in the Bible) and Kabbalistic interpretations of the supposedly different levels of reaching truth and spirituality.

Considering these Jewish styles of interpretation, we can see why Jesus sometimes interpreted the Mosaic Law and other Scriptural texts in the way He did. He often used a simple, literal interpretation, but also a symbolic and allegorical (yet perfectly correct) way of interpreting Scripture. He used the first three styles of *peshat*, *remez*, and *midrash* as tools to explain profound spiritual topics, even when referring to the eschatological resurrection of the saints, the judgment of the unrighteous, and the future Messianic Kingdom. When explaining the meaning and intent of the Law, Jesus usually used everyday speech (*peshat*). He described salvation and correct godly conduct in the same direct manner of earlier Hebrew texts. When describing more complex concepts, such as the equivalent terms of "Kingdom of God" or "Kingdom of Heaven," He usually used symbols and illustrations (*remez*).[47] Jesus used similar symbols and word pictures that the prophets used many years before, and He occasionally used new ones. Among those symbols, Jesus illustrated ordinary people as sheep, the nation of Israel as a fig tree, the Church as a rock, and Himself as the light of the world, the bread of life, etc. Thus, Jesus used simple literal terms as well as symbols to reveal God's truth, whether in past, present, or future terms. Our sense of linguistics and logic must discern the difference between *peshat* and *remez* so that we don't confuse the literal with the symbolic. When Jesus said that we must eat His flesh and drink His blood, which is a *midrashic* representation, those who couldn't see the proper spiritual interpretation were scandalized by His teachings and decided to not follow Him anymore (Jn. 6:51-66).

Jesus once refuted the Sadducees and evidenced the resurrection of the dead by simply referring to God as the father of Abraham, Isaac, and Jacob, who is God *"of the living."*

> *"And as for the dead being raised, have you not read in the book of Moses, in the passage about the bush, how God spoke to him, saying, 'I am the God of Abraham, and the God of Isaac, and the God of Jacob?' He is not God of the dead, but of the living. You are quite wrong"* (Mk. 12:26-27).

This type of interpretation of the Biblical text as valid proof for the resurrection of the dead can seem to us a bit illogical. Yet this was not argued by the Sadducees, because *remez* was already

---

[47] Even though some people see a difference between these two types of kingdoms, Jesus used the terms interchangeably, describing either the individual condition of salvation that people can possess in a present sense through faith in Him as the Son of God, or our ultimate collective salvation that will find its fulfillment in the end of days.

an accepted hermeneutical practice of their time. In contrast, Jesus criticized the teachers of His day when they applied the Law in ways outside of its intended meaning, creating a whole series of traditions that were not pleasing to God. The Pharisees and Sadducees often used *eisegetical* methods of interpretation in order to impose their unbiblical and legalistic requirements on people, while Jesus used a proper *exegetical* method of uniting various Biblical ideas to produce a valid conclusion.

The apostles Peter, Paul and John also used these three Jewish tools of interpretation. Sometimes they would use everyday language to convey their message (*peshat*); at other times they would use symbolism taken from the ancient Hebrew Scriptures, or more modern ones, in order to validate their theology (*remez*); and at other times they used the accepted method of *midrash* to illustrate their profound message in a more story-like manner. Paul once compared our salvation in Jesus to Abraham's two sons, one born by the slave Hagar and the other by the free woman Sarah:

> *"Now this may be interpreted allegorically: these women are two covenants. One is from Mount Sinai, bearing children for slavery; she is Hagar. Now Hagar is Mount Sinai in Arabia; she corresponds to the present Jerusalem, for she is in slavery with her children. But the Jerusalem above is free, and she is our mother. For it is written, 'Rejoice, O barren one who does not bear; break forth and cry aloud, you who are not in labor! For the children of the desolate one will be more than those of the one who has a husband'"* (Gal. 4:24-27).

Paul provided the proper interpretation to his own allegory by referring to Isaiah 54:1, which seemingly does not have any relationship to his point. Nevertheless, using the common practice of *midrashic* interpretation, he showed that the numerous children of the New Covenant, or believers in *Yeshua*, were of a more spiritual nature than those of the Old Covenant since they were born by the Spirit as children of God. Even though many erroneous conclusions have been drawn from this allegory, proper hermeneutics of the text should consider other similar comparisons that Paul made between the Old Covenant and the New Covenant. Even though Paul at times stated that Christians are not *"under the Law"* (Gal 5:18), he was just trying to say that our works in obedience to the Law (*Torah*) do not justify us before God because we are justified only by our faith in Jesus. But salvation was also by faith **before** the cross just as much as **after** the cross (Heb. 4:2). His general message was that *"in Christ Jesus neither circumcision nor uncircumcision counts for anything, but only faith working through love"* (Gal. 5:6). In the end, our faith is evidenced by our works.

Thus, each of Paul's discussions regarding faith versus law should be studied and analyzed together, so that we can come to a proper and unified interpretation of this issue, and not conclude that there is a separation of dispensations between the Law and Grace, which I believe is totally wrong. Evidently, the various positions in this regard demonstrate that not everyone is using correct Christian and Jewish rules of hermeneutics, thus producing much false doctrine in the Church. Using these texts in a wrong manner has sometimes led to a rejection of the Mosaic Law in its entirety, when that was not Paul's intention. He wanted us to value the freedom that Jesus gives us through the New Covenant, because He fulfills the Old Covenant within us through the Holy Spirit. There is no separation of dispensations between the time before the cross and after the cross, because Jesus links all time together in His fulfillment of all things.

Fundamental Principles to the Eschatological Jigsaw Puzzle

To reach a correct hermeneutically and scripturally-sound visualization of God's eschatological picture, I will use the analogy of a common jigsaw puzzle. Usually, when people intend to put together the pieces of a jigsaw puzzle, the box includes a final picture that should guide them along the way. The problem with Biblical eschatology is that we don't have this advantage, and the pieces are distributed throughout all the ancient texts with no chronological order to them. This was also the problem when Jesus' disciples needed to put together the picture of the prophetic Scriptures regarding His first coming. Those pieces are distributed all over the Old Testament as well, and only through Jesus' teachings and the inspiration of the Holy Spirit were the early believers and Gospel writers able to extract them and place them in a coherent picture. Due to this confusing situation, many theories have been put forth by sincere and earnest Christians and Jews, but with diametrically opposing conclusions. Evidently, some theories have to be totally wrong, and others might be only partially right or wrong.

But, can we assume that there is only **one** truth regarding eschatology, just as there is only one truth regarding any of the other Biblical doctrines, or can we be satisfied with such a diverse collection of opinions? Is it possible that God doesn't mind that Scripture be interpreted in varying ways, depending on personal preferences? Are we allowed to each have our own view of who God is and what His ultimate goal is for humankind? More importantly, would God want to leave us in our ignorance if it were important that we know the truth?

I say "no" to all the above questions. My goal is that we obtain complete truth. That is my aim. I believe that we should each strive to reach God's pure and unadulterated truth in spite of our limited human mind. He wants to reveal to us the truth through His Word, and in that way the Body of Christ can reach a fuller understanding of Him. God is *"making known to us the **mystery of his will**, according to his purpose, which he set forth in Christ as a **plan for the fullness of time**, to unite all things in him, things in heaven and things on earth"* (Eph. 1:9-10). Jesus is the center of all God's plans, and everything will ultimately be united in Him. He is revealing His mysterious will to us regarding the fullness of time, specifically His eschatological plan. Even if we might be wrong in some of the details, I believe that we should make our best effort to understanding God's plans and purposes for His people, not only for the present time, but also regarding future days. This should be based on the trustworthy Word of God, a bountiful collection of writings inspired by the Holy Spirit. Those should be our starting point for any understanding of God and the end-times. Its eternal principles should provide us with a correct outer framework for this eschatological puzzle, plus the way in which the smaller pieces fit around the main centerpieces.

Thus, I will initially identify a series of foundational principles that should provide us with the outer framework for putting together this eschatological puzzle, and hopefully avoid falling captive to a great number of possible deceptions. These are the most foundational and non-negotiable premises that I trust will guide us for later analysis. These Biblical premises will produce the outer "corners," "borders," and "centerpieces" of the eschatological puzzle so that all the other pieces can fall together better into place.

A very crucial aspect of my hermeneutics is based on a **continuous yet progressive** perspective of salvation history, beginning with the origins of mankind until reaching the fulfillment of all things, rather than on a discontinuous dispensationalist view of different "economies." A continuous and gradually expanding revelation makes much more Biblical sense, since God has never changed His plans nor His ways of dealing with mankind. It is true that people have understood God in different ways down through history, but He has continued to reveal Himself more abundantly with the passing of time to those who seek Him and to those who desire to live according to His perfect will.

The most crucial and eternal Biblical truth that should give a solid foundation in order to define the borders of this eschatological puzzle is that **both Jews and Christians will ultimately form "one new man,"** according to Ephesians 2:15, which has always been the focus of God's eternal purposes with mankind since the creation of this world. Satan has been trying to impede His people from reaching this goal, but the real people of God should be sensitive to His leading and allow Him to take us where He wants.

> "For he himself is our peace, who **has made us both one** and has broken down in his flesh the dividing wall of hostility…that he might create in himself **one new man in place of the two**,…but you are fellow citizens with

the saints and members of the household of God, built on the foundation of the apostles and prophets…" (Eph. 2:13-22).

God's unending Covenant with Israel and the Church's union with the Jewish people through the New Covenant is crucial in the eschatological debate and the timing of the resurrection of His saints. While the Pretribulational rapture theory places the Church **without** Israel at the "rapture" or resurrection (as well as most other theories), God's eternal purposes in **uniting Israel and the Church** should be the main centerpiece of any Biblically solid end-time theology. The Church has had the privilege of being grafted into God's Covenant with the Jewish people through Jesus' atonement for all who would believe in Him (Rom. 11). In the books of the **Old Testament** we find descriptions of God's eternal Covenant made with Israel, plus later prophetic pronouncements of a New Covenant that He would make with Israel in order to include the Gentiles (Jer. 31:31; Heb. 9:15). God told the Jewish people about a physical resurrection of the righteous for eternal life and of the unrighteous for eternal condemnation (Dan. 12:1-2), plus a return to an Edenic-type Millennial Kingdom (Isa. 60:1-18) and then a new heaven and new earth with Jerusalem as God's Holy Mountain (Isa. 60:19-20, 65:17-25), just He told the Gentile believers that were later included through the New Covenant.

Critically, the **New Testament** confirms and upholds those Old Testament promises, and does not disqualify the Jews from seeing their fulfillment, as it says in Luke 1:32-33 about Jesus: *"…And the Lord God will give to him the throne of his father David, and **he will reign over the house of Jacob forever**, and of his kingdom there will be no end."* The Church does not replace Israel in God's plans, but His purpose is to see Israel and the Church united in a common future, without denoting a preference for one above the other (Eph. 2:13-16).

Undoubtedly, since *"flesh and blood cannot inherit the Kingdom of God"* (1 Cor. 15:50), this requires that Israel believe in its Messiah before the resurrection of the saints so that it can receive its promised Kingdom. As Paul stated in Romans 11:26-27: *"And in this way **all Israel will be saved**, as it is written, 'The Deliverer will come from Zion, he will banish ungodliness from Jacob; and this will be my covenant with them when I take away their sins.'"* **But the Church will not be raised without Israel, nor Israel without the Church.** We will all be one spiritual body at the time of the resurrection. If an end-time theory does not have Jews and Christians together for this event, there is something fundamentally wrong with the picture.

God has always had this eternal principle in mind, which is part and parcel of His character as well as of His purposes. This non-negotiable principle should be the "main centerpiece" of our eschatological theory so that we can be confident that the picture will end up true to God's final picture. Below, I will first identify the four basic "corners" of the puzzle that have to do with God's eternal promises for all His people, and then identify the four fundamental "sides" that have to do with His eternal plans, which together form the boundary or framework of God's eschatology.

A. Four "Corners" of the Puzzle

According to the above fundamental Biblical premise, I distinguish four essential "corners" as indisputable truths in God's eschatology regarding all His people, both Jewish and Christian:

1) God's OT saints and present-day Jews are still God's people.

God still sees the Old Testament Israelites and present-day Jews as part of His people. He said: *"If the heavens above can be measured, and the foundations of the earth below can be explored, then I will cast off all the offspring of Israel for all that they have done"* (Jer. 31:37). Evidently, this is not possible, so God will never cast off His people, even though some Christians may think that God has already discarded them. And even if they have not yet believed in the Messiah, they are still God's people, and eventually they will believe:

> *"For this is the covenant that I will make with the house of Israel after those days, declares the LORD:* **I will put my law within them,** *and I will write it on their hearts. And I will be their God, and they shall be my people"* (Jer. 31:33).

And when the nation of Israel believes, it will also be filled with the Holy Spirit:

> *"'And as for me, this is my covenant with them,' says the LORD:* **'My Spirit that is upon you,** *and my words that I have put in your mouth, shall not depart out of your mouth, or out of the mouth of your offspring, or out of the mouth of your children's offspring,' says the LORD, 'from this time forth and forevermore'"* (Isa. 59:21).

2) The Church is included in God's New Covenant with Israel.

God said He would make a New Covenant with Israel (Jer. 31:31-34), but it was also going to include the Gentiles by faith in Israel's Messiah (Heb. 9:15-18). Since Isaiah spoke of a "new thing" that would include the "coastlands" in His Covenant (Isa. 42:1-9; 49:1-6; 51:4-5), the events that are prophesied for one group will also include the other. Foreigners will join the Jews in God's house of prayer (Isa. 56:8b), and many nations will join themselves to the Lord and together become His holy people (Zech. 2:10-11), having one flock under one Shepherd (Jn. 10:16). And even though the Jews have stumbled and not yet received their Messiah as a whole, *"through their trespass salvation has come to the Gentiles, to make Israel jealous"* (Rom. 11:11). We can be thankful for their trespass, yet compassionate so as to love them and accept them, as God does.

3) God has partially fulfilled His promises regarding Israel's land.

We must never think that Israel will have to suffer a worse tribulation than it has so far. God has already removed from Israel's hand the bowl of His wrath: *"…Behold, I have taken from your hand the cup of staggering; the bowl of my wrath you shall drink no more; and I will put it into the hand of your tormentors…"* (Isa. 51:22-23). Never again will they hear the reproach of the nations or be disgraced (Ezek. 36:15).

> *"I will take you from the nations and gather you from all the countries and* **bring you into your own land***. I will sprinkle clean water on you, and you shall be clean from all*

your uncleanness, and from all your idols I will cleanse you"
(Ezek. 36:24-25).

This process began in the 19th century, and continues until today. As stated above, we are still waiting for Israel to have a new heart and a new spirit (v. 26-27), but this is the next part of the promise. *"And even they, if they do not continue in their unbelief, will be grafted in* [to their own olive tree], *for God has the power to* **graft them in again***"* (Rom. 11:23). God is faithful to His chosen nation, and will ultimately do as He said He would do.

4) **God will keep His promises of resurrection and the Kingdom.**

God also promised that Israel's saints will experience a physical resurrection in the latter days:

> *"Your dead shall live; their bodies shall rise. You who dwell in the dust, awake and sing for joy! For your dew is a dew of light, and the earth will give birth to the dead"* (Isa. 26:19).

We should also consider Deut. 32:99, 1 Sam. 2:6; Isa. 25:6-8, Job 19:25-27, Ps. 17:15, Ezek. 37:12-14, Hos. 13:14 as evidence of God's promises of resurrection for the Jewish people. All His Old Testament saints will be delivered, though it is qualified by: *"**everyone whose name** shall be found written in the book"* (Dan. 12:1), and they will finally possess the kingdom (Dan. 7:22).

B. Four "Sides" of the Puzzle

On the other hand, the four basic "sides" to the eschatological puzzle are the truths regarding His eternal purposes, and can be understood to be the following:

1) Resurrection of New Covenant Saints (1st Resurrection)

This promise of bodily resurrection from the dead is for **all saints** of the Old Testament and the New Testament thanks to the New Covenant that God made with both the Jews and the Gentiles. A correct order of final events cannot leave them behind. God never talks about one resurrection for the Jews and a different one for the Christians. This will include Old Testament saints such as King David, the prophet Daniel, and Abraham, who were **looking forward by faith** to the Messiah and hoping for a better homeland (Heb. 11:10, 13-16). According to Jesus, *"...**everyone who looks on the Son** and believes in him should have eternal life, and I will **raise him up on the last day**"* (Jn. 6:40). But this believing should be much more than just a mental acknowledgment, because God's Spirit must be indwelling:

> *"**If the Spirit of him** who raised Jesus from the dead **dwells in you**, he who raised Christ Jesus from the dead **will also give life to your mortal bodies** through his Spirit who dwells in you"* (Rom. 8:11).

This indwelling of God's Spirit is also a requirement for anyone to receive an immortal body at the time of the resurrection, whether Jew or Gentile.

2) Messianic Millennial Kingdom

"In the regeneration (KJV) or *"in the new world"* (ESV), the Son of Man will sit on His glorious throne, and His disciples will sit on 12 thrones (the original 11 Jewish believers, minus Judas, plus Matthias), judging the 12 tribes of Israel (Matt. 19:28-29). Other believers will also have a position of authority, yet none will be greater than any other, since all will be equal in the Kingdom and will co-reign with Abraham, Isaac, and Jacob (Matt. 8:11).

> *"Then I saw thrones and seated on them were those* **to whom the authority to judge was committed**...*They came to life and reigned with Christ for a thousand years"* (Rev. 20:4).

Moreover, those who are raised to life *"cannot die anymore, because they are equal to angels and are sons of God, being sons of the resurrection"* (Lk. 20:35-36), in contrast with those who will not be raised to life.

3) Judgment of Unbelievers (2ⁿᵈ Resurrection)

At *"the end of the age"* (or at the end of the Messianic Kingdom), the "Son of Man" and His angels will gather all the remaining sinners for their eternal punishment. These are the ones who never participated in the First Resurrection (Matt. 13:39-42; Rev. 20:5-6). At this moment, the **weeds** will be gathered **before the harvest**, and thrown into the fiery furnace. Then the righteous will shine like the sun in the new and everlasting kingdom of the Father.

> *"The Son of Man will send his angels, and they will* **gather out of his kingdom all causes of sin and all**

law-breakers, and throw them into the fiery furnace. In that place there will be weeping and gnashing of teeth. Then the righteous will shine like the sun in the kingdom of their Father. He who has ears, let him hear" (Matt. 13:41-43).

4) The Father's Eternal Kingdom (New Heaven and New Earth)

As seen above, the righteous "sons of the Kingdom" (Matt. 13:38) will shine like the sun in the Father's eternal Kingdom (Matt. 13:43). This will be when God makes a new heaven and a new earth for all His people:

> *"For as the new heavens and the new earth that I make shall remain before me, says the LORD, so shall your offspring and your name remain"* (Isa. 66:22).

> *"Then I saw a new heaven and a new earth, for the first heaven and the first earth had passed away, and the sea was no more"* (Rev. 21:1).

We can now look at an illustration of my proposed border for God's eschatological puzzle using the essential four "corners" and four "sides" described above, which I perceive as non-negotiable Biblical truths. In the center is the main centerpiece that also forms part of this eschatological position. The timing and sequence of other end-time events is one of the most difficult issues to resolve, but everything should be within the constraints of this basic framework and centerpiece, so that the final picture will not be skewed.

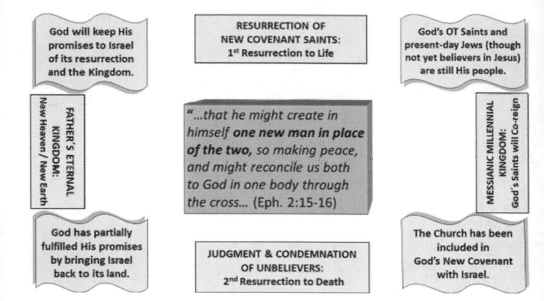

Now we can continue to fill in the picture of God's eschatological puzzle regarding some of the most difficult areas, which will be the main focus of this book.

7

Redefining Important Concepts

A. Great Tribulation vs. Normal Tribulations

1) Great Tribulation

For the pieces of the eschatological puzzle to fall into place in relation to the resurrection of the saints and the so-called "Great Tribulation," we must start by rethinking and redefining the concept of "Great Tribulation." According to most interpretations regarding the last and missing piece of Daniel's 70 weeks (Dan. 9:27), this will be a future and literal 7-year period. Pretribulationists understand that there has been an "interruption in God's clock," or a pause in God's intervention with mankind, since the ending of the 69th week. But, as defended previously, it is more Biblically reasonable to say that God is extending time in order to have mercy on more people rather than stopping the clock (2 Pet. 3:8-9). He is not in any hurry when it comes to extending His wrath against so many blind and confused people. He wants to make sure that everyone has had a fair opportunity to repent before that time, and we are to use this time to spread the message of the Gospel of salvation unto all the world.

In addition, God told Daniel that the revelations he received would at first be sealed from human understanding, *"for the words are shut up and sealed **until the time of the end**"* (Dan. 12:9). I believe that **now** is the time for a correct understanding.

Because of Daniel's mysterious last "week," many Christians have interpreted apocalyptic time references in a distorted way with the hope that they will miss certain horrible events that they think are in the near future. But what if the terrible days of "Great Tribulation" that Jesus referred to have already passed, even though some normal tribulations have still been ongoing for centuries? As stated before, we should be careful when interpreting apocalyptic numerical time references, because they might only represent certain foundational spiritual truths. For example, the number 7 is a representation for completeness, and when it is multiplied by 10 it represents the utmost amplification of God's perfection and holy purposes. Jesus told us to forgive those who offend us 70 times 7 (Matt. 18:22). That is also why the angel told Daniel that the ultimate everlasting righteousness is to be reached after 70 "weeks" (Dan. 9:24).

If we consider this last "week" of Daniel in an extended sense rather than in a literal sense, we can see that many Biblical prophecies have already been fulfilled.

Clearly, Jesus warned about a time of **great distress and tribulation** referring to the destruction of the Temple in Jerusalem, the dispersion of the Jewish people, and the establishment of an abomination of desolations on the Temple Mount. He never said that this would last only seven years, but rather that the Temple would be trampled **until the times of the Gentiles is fulfilled**.

*"So when you see the abomination of desolation spoken of by the prophet Daniel, standing in the holy place...**then** there will*

be ***great tribulation*** [megas thlipsis], *such as has not been from the beginning of the world until now, no, and never will be"* (Matt. 24:15, 21).

*"But when you see the abomination of desolation standing where he ought not to be...**in those days** there will be such tribulation* [megas thlipsis] *as has not been from the beginning of the creation that God created until now, and never will be"* (Mark 13:14, 19).

*"But when you see Jerusalem surrounded by armies, then know that its desolation has come **near**...For there will be **great distress*** [megas anangké] *upon the earth and wrath against **this people**. They will fall by the edge of the sword and be led captive among all nations, and Jerusalem will be trampled underfoot by the Gentiles, **until the times of the Gentiles are fulfilled***" (Lk. 21:20, 23b-24).

The Gospels use the terms "great tribulation" (*megas thlipsis*, in Matthew and Mark) and "great distress" (*megas anangké*, in Luke) when describing this terrible destruction of Jerusalem, the dispersion of the Jewish people, and also the abomination of desolations upon the Temple Mount. It would be greater than any **previous** or even **later** tribulations, which clearly implies that there will be more tribulations after that. Those tribulations that Jesus referred to represent the most catastrophic events in all of Jewish history, even if we compare them to early Biblical times and to more recent times. Their first exile in Babylon only lasted around 70 years, but the Jewish dispersion that began in the 1st and 2nd centuries did not end until the middle of the 20th century, not until **after** the intense Nazi Holocaust was unleashed against the Jews. I believe that this Roman eviction of the

Jewish nation from their land in AD 70 is what Jesus meant as the *"megas thlipsis"* or "great tribulation" This could be the equivalent to **"Jacob's Trouble"** (Jer. 30:7, KJV), their worldwide dispersion and persecution, after which they would be saved "from far away."

> *"Alas!* **That day** *is so great there is none like it; it is a* **time of distress for Jacob;** *yet he shall be* **saved out of it.** *And it shall come to pass in that day, declares the LORD of hosts, that I will break his yoke from off your neck, and I will burst your bonds, and* **foreigners shall no more make a servant of him.** *But they shall serve the LORD their God and* **David their king, whom I will raise up for them.** *Then fear not, O Jacob my servant, declares the LORD, nor be dismayed, O Israel; for behold, I* **will save you from far away,** *and your offspring from the land of their captivity.* **Jacob shall return and have quiet and ease,** *and none shall make him afraid"* (Jer. 30:7-10).

It is interesting to note that this verse says they will serve the Lord their God and David their king, whom God would raise up for them, a very clear reference to Jesus' resurrection from the dead. God will bring them back from their captivity and make them live in quiet and ease. It is debatable whether they actually live in quiet and ease, but the nation has grown so strong that they fear no one, while they are always defensive and watchful of their enemies. In any case, there is a direct link between Israel returning to its land and their salvation through David their King.

Daniel was also warned about a period of **great tribulation** for His people such as had never occurred before, though most Bibles use other terms, such as "trouble": *"And there shall be a time of* **trouble**

[tzarah, equivalent to tribulation], *such as never has been since there was a nation till that time...."* (Dan. 12:1a). The text immediately continues saying: *"But **at that time** your people shall be delivered..."* which does not necessarily refer to the same immediate moment, but could refer to an undetermined later time. In any case, Daniel's people (the Jews) would be finally delivered (*malat*), which also means a leaping out or rescuing from a place. Thus, that deliverance could refer to a physical return to their land, but also an "awakening" of those who sleep in the dust at a later time, an evident reference to the resurrection of the saints: *"...But **at that time** your people shall be delivered, everyone whose name shall be found written in the book. And many of those who sleep in the dust of the earth **shall awake**, some **to everlasting life**, and some to shame and everlasting contempt"* (Dan. 12:1b-2). All the events described here are quite squeezed together, since it does not reveal any lapse of time between the physical return to the land, the first resurrection (for everlasting life) nor the second resurrection (for everlasting contempt). Other Bible texts clarify that the Jews would return to their own land, and later there would be a first resurrection of the righteous before the thousand year Messianic Kingdom, and finally a second one for the unrighteous. The above verse is just the quick snapshot of the whole final scenario.

It should be noted that a *"man clothed in linen"* then told Daniel there would be a lapse of time between when the Temple would be destroyed and the Abomination of Desolations would be established: *"And from the time that the regular burnt offering is taken away and the* **abomination that makes desolate is set up**, *there shall be **1,290 days**"* (Dan. 12:11). Historically, there was a time gap of about 620 years between the destruction of the Temple and when the Muslims established their mosque on God's holy mountain, not merely 1,290 days. Again, we must avoid being literal regarding the time references in apocalyptic writings.

Daniel 12:7 also clarifies that Israel's tribulations would not finish until the shattering of God's people has ended, implying a very long time: *"...it would be for a time, times, and half a time, and that when the* **shattering of the power of the holy people comes to an end** *all these things would be finished"* (Dan. 12:7). The "man in linen" added:

> *"**Many** shall **purify themselves** and make themselves white and be refined, but the wicked shall act wickedly. And none of the wicked shall understand, but **those who are wise shall understand**"* (Dan. 12:10).

I believe that the above term "many" is very significant, since "many" is also used in reference to Jesus making *"**many** to be accounted righteous"* (Isaiah 53:11) after bearing *"the sins of **many**"* (Isaiah 53:12). These "many" will be purified and refined, and will also "understand" once they are made wise. Then Daniel 12:12 adds: *"Blessed is he who waits and arrives at the **1,335 days**,"* which is literally only 45 days after the previous 1,290 days. This last reference seems to represent a special blessing, perhaps the long-expected day of resurrection of the saints, as Daniel was promised his own resurrection at the end of days (Dan. 12:13).

In short, I believe that we can safely assume that what is meant by the term "great tribulation" is really the terrible disaster that occurred to the Jewish people in the year AD 70 and their nearly 2,000-year dispersion. More importantly, it seems like that time is already over! Perhaps we can say that the times of the Gentiles reached its completion when the Jews began to experience the fulfillment of God's promises as they returned to their land and when their nation finally became restored in 1948. They still only have partial control over the Temple Mount, but no longer do the Gentiles treat them as servants, nor do Gentiles control the land of Israel. Admittedly, Israel is still surrounded by hostile Muslim nations that want to take it over, and most other nations still don't feel very sympathetic to the Jews, so the ancient anti-Semitism has not yet disappeared. But the Jews live in their land by God's power, and the rest of the world admires and respects them, though they might also resent them, as they may resent the God of Israel.

Thus, the Pretribulationists' dread of a future "Great Tribulation" for Christians that they hope to miss because of the "rapture" is totally unwarranted!

2) **Normal Tribulations, Signs, and Wrath**

On the other hand, Jesus also said that in this world Christians would have tribulation: *"I have said these things to you, that in me you may have peace. In the world you will have **tribulation** [thlipsis]…"* (Jn. 16:33). This world would always be a source of tribulation for Christians, yet we would find peace in Him. The term "tribulation" is a translation of the Greek term *thlipsis*, but the Greek word appears much more often than the English term is actually used. Bible translators seem to prefer terms other than "tribulation" when it doesn't have to do with their preconceived notions of the seven-year "Tribulation." For example, Paul used *thlipsis* in 2 Corinthians 4:8-9 and 17-18 regarding Christian's present sufferings, and he referred to these tribulations as something momentary that were preparing them for a future glory. The ESV below translates this word as "afflictions" rather than "tribulations":

> *"We are **afflicted** [an adverbial form of thlipsis] in every way, but not crushed; perplexed, but not driven to despair;*

persecuted, but not forsaken; struck down, but not destroyed; ...
*For this light momentary **affliction** [thlipsis] is preparing*
for us an eternal weight of glory beyond all comparison, as we
look not to the things that are seen but to the things that are
unseen" (2 Cor. 4:8-9, 17-18).

Paul clarified that Christians would experiment "tribulation" because God would allow it, *"so that the life of Jesus also may be manifested in our mortal flesh"* (v. 11). These life-long tribulations are preparing us for our future resurrection and eternal life in God's Kingdom.

In contrast with the term *thlipsis* used by Matthew and Mark in their Olivet Discourse, Luke used *anangké* in his account about Israel's tribulations (Luke 21:23), which can also be translated as "distress," "anguish," or "calamity": *"For there will be great distress [anangké] upon the earth and **wrath against this people**."* (Note that Israel wouldn't be the only nation to suffer the wrath of the Roman Empire, but that the "earth," or the known world surrounding Israel, would too.) Paul used the term *anangké* when he wrote to the Thessalonians about his afflictions: *"...in all our distress [thlipsis] and affliction [anangké] we have been comforted about you through your faith"* (1 Thess. 3:7). Here, both are used in a synonymous way and mean tribulations. Maybe distress could be more emotional, while affliction could be more physical, but they both refer to tribulations.

Jesus also clarified what **type** of tribulation the Christians could expect:

> *"Then they will deliver you up to **tribulation** and put you to death, and you will be **hated by all nations for my name's sake**"* (Matt. 24:9).

*"And because **lawlessness** will be increased, the love of many will grow cold. But the one who **endures to the end** will be saved. And this **gospel of the kingdom** will be proclaimed throughout the whole world as a testimony to all nations, and **then the end will come**"* (Matt. 24:12-14).

We can't deny that Christians have always been experiencing "normal tribulations" due to opposition of their faith in midst of a Godless environment. These were to be something "normal" that all Christians would experience. Paul told Timothy: *"Indeed, all who desire to live a godly life in Christ Jesus will be persecuted, while evil people and impostors will go on from bad to worse, deceiving and being deceived"* (2 Tim. 3:12-13). Nevertheless, these tribulations can be tolerated in hope, patience, and prayer. *"Rejoice in hope, **be patient in tribulation**, be constant in prayer"* (Rom. 12:12).

Christians are still being martyred in many countries around the world, mostly in Muslim-controlled countries, even though we may not be experiencing it in "Christian nations." Daniel declared that, though the "wise" of God's people (which can include both Christians and Jews) would stumble and suffer persecution, they should remain firm "for some days" until the appointed time of the end.

*"...though **for some days** they shall stumble by sword and flame, by captivity and plunder...so that they may be refined, purified, and made white, **until the time of the end**, for it still awaits **the appointed time**"* (Dan. 11:33-35).

Daniel 7:12 also refers to a similar extension or prolongation of time regarding some beasts through the enigmatic phrase *"for a season and a time."* It reads: *"As for the rest of the **beasts**, their dominion was taken* *away, but **their lives were prolonged for a season and a time***" (Dan. 7:12). This says that several beasts will have dominion and would fall, but that "their lives" will be prolonged for an indefinite time. If the lives of these beasts are prolonged, why and for how long is that? This issue of the beasts will be discussed later, but what is important to see here is that it is definitely a lengthening of time, not an interruption of time. Jesus even said: *"Be on guard, keep awake. For you do not know when the time will come"* (Mk. 13:33).

In addition, can we say that these tribulations are only meant for the Jews and Christians? In the verses that precede and follow Jesus' description in the Synoptic Gospels about the Temple and the Jewish people, He spoke about other things that needed to occur **on a global scale** and for an extended period of time to **all inhabitants** of the earth. I believe that the order in which Jesus described these struggles and tribulations does not reflect a chronological sequence of events. These "tribulations" have been taking place for the past almost 20 centuries, such as wars, famines, diseases, and upheavals in nature, and will continue to do so until the end. In my estimation, these general global events correspond to the first **five "Seals"** of Revelation, things that are to be experienced by all people. More importantly, Jesus never said that these things would occur in only a matter of seven years, but that they would be the *"beginning of birth pains"* the world over. And **even then**, the end was not yet to come.

> *"And you will hear of wars and rumors of wars. See that you are not alarmed, for this must take place, but **the end is not yet**. For nation will rise against nation, and kingdom against kingdom, and there will be famines and earthquakes in various places. All these are but the **beginning of the birth pains**"* (Matt. 24:6-8).

Another important issue is the expectancy of **divine signs,** which are of great importance to the Jews in order for them to recognize the true Messiah. After describing the destruction of the Temple, Jesus' disciples asked Him: *"Teacher, when will these things be, and what will be the **sign** when these things are about to take place?"* (Lk. 21:7). Jesus described His long list of terrible things, but then He spoke about the signs right before He is to appear in the clouds. Here we find the word *sunoché* (in Luke 21:25), translated by the ESV as "distress," term that also signifies "anxiety." It points to how the **unbelieving people** will be so stressed-out during the "signs" that precede Jesus' appearance that they will be fainting with fear and foreboding.

> *"And there will be **signs** in sun and moon and stars, and on the earth **distress** [sunoché] of nations in perplexity because of the roaring of the sea and the waves, people fainting with fear and with foreboding of what is coming on the world. For the powers of the heavens will be shaken. And **then they will see the Son of Man coming in a cloud** with power and great glory"* (Lk. 21:25-27).

Matthew uses the term **"tribulation of those days,"** after which we will see those signs, including the **"sign of the Son of Man"** (Matt. 24:29). Jesus added: *"So also, when you see these things taking place, you know that the kingdom of God is near"* (Lk. 21:31).

Actually, these signs before Jesus' appearance are different from "normal *thlipsis*," since they are heavenly events caused by God that will cause enormous anxiety and perplexity among the unsaved. In fact, most normal tribulations are caused by man's inhumanity to man, induced by Satan. But the above "signs" should actually give

Christians comfort, hope and rejoicing, as they can recognize that the day of their redemption is drawing near.

Revelation 6:12-17 describes some of these "signs" in the Sixth Seal:

> "When he opened the **sixth seal**, I looked, and behold, there was a great earthquake, and the sun became black as sackcloth, the full moon became like blood, and the stars of the sky fell to the earth as the fig tree sheds its winter fruit when shaken by a gale. The sky vanished like a scroll that is being rolled up, and every mountain and island was removed from its place. Then the **kings of the earth** and the great ones and the generals and **the rich and the powerful**, and **everyone**, slave and free, hid themselves in the caves and among the rocks of the mountains, calling to the mountains and rocks, 'Fall on us and hide us from the face of him who is seated on the throne, and from the **wrath of the Lamb**, for the **great day of their wrath** [οργη, orgé] has come, and who can stand?'" (Rev. 6:12-17).

Even though unbelievers will think that the day of the Lamb's wrath has arrived, it will be merely a glimpse of the future Bowls of Wrath [θυμος, *thumós*] that they will experience once God's people have been raised and taken out of the way. Most Midtribulationists believe that this Sixth Seal marks the middle of the literal seven-year Tribulation and the beginning of the terrible "Day of the Lord." Nevertheless, the wrath will not yet begin at this point.

Etymologically, *orgé* mainly refers to the **contained emotion** of anger, while *thumós* refers to the passionate and **fierce expression** of that anger. God's *thumós* will be an expression of His *orgé*. That is why the Bowls of Wrath (*thumós*) are different from this sample of

God's anger (*orgé*) of the Sixth Seal. Yet the words can also be used together, as when *"God remembered Babylon the great, to make her drain the cup of the wine of the* **fury** *[thumós] of his* **wrath** *[orgé]"* (Rev. 16:19), where both are used together, translated by the ESV as *"the fury of his wrath."*

I believe that Revelation's Sixth and Seventh Seals are probably a **united uninterrupted** period, which will also include the Seven Trumpets. These "trumpets" will be announcing global upheavals in nature as well as worse tyrannical oppression. We don't know how long this time will last, but these could represent what Jesus described as the **"tribulation of those days."** (This will be addressed in more detail later.) But God's *thumós* is reserved only for the unbelievers after the last Trumpet.

God's people are told to **hide away for a while** and to expect His protection during a time of God's *orgé*, as the prophet Isaiah says: *"Come, my people, enter your chambers, and shut your doors behind you; hide yourselves for a little while until the fury* [orgé, in the Septuagint] *has passed by"* (Isa. 26:20). This verse is sandwiched between a clear and acknowledged reference to the resurrection: *"Your dead shall live; their bodies shall rise…"* (Isa. 26:19) and God's plan to punish evildoers: *"… The LORD is coming out from his place to punish the inhabitants of the earth for their iniquity"* (Isa. 26:21).

Does the order of these three verses indicate a necessary chronological order of events? Not at all. If we look at verse 16 of the same chapter, we read: *"O LORD, in* **distress** *[tzar] they sought you; they poured out a whispered prayer when your* **discipline** *[musar] was upon them."* This indicates a tribulation that God will allow upon the nation of Israel as He disciplines them, during which time they will pray and seek God. It would be like the pains of a woman giving birth (Isa.

26:17-18), but it would be God's chastisement so as to obtain their repentance.

The next verse is the mentioned reference to the resurrection of the dead, the call for His people to hide, and then the warning to the rest of the inhabitants of the earth that God is going to punish the inhabitants for their iniquity. We can interpret that God was reminding Israel of His promise of resurrection before telling them that it would take some time, but His plan was to ultimately vindicate them. This time of hiding could represent God's *"orgé"* before the resurrection of the saints, symbolized by the Sixth Seal and the first Six Trumpets. God's *thumós*, or His expression of wrath, will actually come upon the remaining nations after the resurrection.

We must always remember that God can protect us in the midst of our present tribulations. This was experienced by the Israelites when they suffered several of the first plagues together with the Egyptians, but were protected from the last of them in the land of Goshen. They were especially shielded by the blood of the sacrificed lamb during the very last plague, which was right before God took them out of Egypt. They were taken *"up out"* of the land in victory (Ex. 3:8), an illustration of the physical resurrection from the dead **at the end** of the plagues.

Returning to the topic of the Sixth and Seventh Seals, and as stated before, I believe that this represents a foretaste and warning to unbelievers about the Bowls of Wrath that are to follow, and which are meant only for them. Christians will be experiencing at least a minimum amount of torment from these "seals" and the subsequent "Six Trumpets" along with unbelievers, but they may also be protected and cared for by God. Then on the blessed *"last day"* (Jn. 6:40), right before the **Seventh Trumpet**, Jesus will appear to gather up His people, both Christians and Jews, and take them to

Himself to celebrate the Marriage Feast. This is when I believe the Antichrist, whose spirit is already now manifested in the world, will take over the Holy Land and most of the global institutions, since there won't be any spiritual opposition to his dominion. (This will also be discussed in more detail later.)

We should remember that Jesus said all these things so that we would not become fearful, because we can have **peace in Him**! And when He spoke of the day of the resurrection of the saints, He termed it *"the last day"*: *"And this is the will of him who sent me, that I should lose nothing of all that he has given me, but raise it up on the last day"* (Jn. 6:39, also 40, 44, 54). He was not indicating a dreadful day but a **wonderful day**, implying that the resurrection would occur at the end of the **"tribulation of those days"** and that our suffering would be over at that point. He wants us to look forward to this day with joy and peace, not with sorrow, desperation, or fear.

Nevertheless, we are called to **endure this suffering until the end**, another implication of an extension of time. When Jesus told His disciples that *"...the one who **endures to the end** will be saved"* (Mk. 13:13; Matt. 24:13), it clearly also applies to Christians, not just Jews. God knows that when we have endured all we can, it will be time to cut it short: *"But for the sake of **the elect**, whom he chose, he shortened the days"* (Mk. 13:20). God holds time totally in His hands, and He can extend or shorten it as He sees fit. It is also noteworthy that God sees time in a broad global sense, not merely in terms of individual lifetimes. Even though He can focus on individual lives, He also sees humanity in a collective manner, including nations and people groups, and the long-term goal is His major focus.

3) Tribulations of Early Believers

Early believers gave us a wonderful example of how their suffering and tribulations were endured through their faith in Christ. The Epistle of Barnabas is a well-authenticated non-canonical document from the 1st century that speaks about the Christians going through times of tribulation.[48] It was probably written shortly after AD 70 by Barnabas, an emissary of James and an early missionary companion to Paul, as seen in the Acts of the Apostles. It is of such early writing that the author does not use the word Christian but reflects the early Jewish believer's worldview of the Nazorean Israelite movement.[49] He believed that they were already going through the prophetic "tribulation," as many other generations have also done regarding their own time. Barnabas referred to the "beasts" of Daniel 7 and believed that the tribulation would soon end with the breaking down of the Roman Empire. Chapter 4:3 of this epistle says: "The end of the tribulation is at hand. This is written about it: Enoch says, 'For this purpose, YHWH cut short the times and the days so His beloved might hurry and come into his inheritance,'"[50] possibly quoting from the pseudo-epigraphical text of Enoch, and also referring to Jesus' mention of those days being cut short for the sake of the elect (Matt. 24:22).

When Jesus warned us that we would have tribulations in this world, He added after that: "*...But take heart; I have overcome the world*" (Jn. 16:33). The early apostles understood this in a similar fashion because after Paul was stoned almost to death, he bravely declared

---

[48] *Epistle of Barnabas*, trans. Jackson H. Snyder and Theodore Dornan, from Hoole's 1885 translation, http://www.jacksonsnyder.com/_yah/manuscript-library/Bar-Nabba-final-021310.pdf (August 28, 2018).

[49] Ibid, 6.

[50] Ibid, 18.

that *"through many tribulations [thlipsis] we must enter the kingdom of God"* (Acts 14:22). He wrote to the Thessalonians: *"For when we were with you, we kept telling you beforehand that we were to suffer **affliction** [a term related to thlipsis], just as it has come to pass, and just as you know"* (1 Thess. 3:4). Here, the KJV translates it as "tribulation."

Paul also wrote in Romans 5:1-5 that those who have been justified by faith, who have peace with God through our Lord Jesus Christ, can rejoice in their tribulation (*thlipsis*), knowing that suffering produces endurance, character, and hope because God's love has been poured into our hearts through the Holy Spirit. He also told them: *"Who shall separate us from the love of Christ? Shall tribulation [thlipsis], or distress, or persecution, or famine, or nakedness, or danger, or sword?"* (Rom. 8:35). The message was that Christians should expect to suffer tribulation, but we can trust that Jesus will accompany us during all this pain, whether we live or die, and we can take heart because Jesus will ultimately overcome.

Paul told the Thessalonians that he was proud of the way in which they were steadfast and faithful in the persecutions and tribulations (*thlipsis*) that they endured (2 Thess. 1:4). But then he added: *"This is evidence of the righteous judgment of God, that you may be considered worthy of the kingdom of God, for which you are also suffering—since indeed God considers it just to repay with affliction [thlipsis] those who afflict you…"* (2 Thess. 1:5-6). We see here that those who suffer tribulation will be considered worthy of the Kingdom of God, yet God will also avenge their pain in the end because God will repay with affliction those who afflicted them. This emphasizes that Christians will certainly suffer tribulation before their resurrection, but afterwards Christ will come down from heaven with His angels and saints to take vengeance on those who did not obey the Gospel and to punish them with everlasting destruction (2 Thess. 1:7-10). Here, Paul is referring to the time following the resurrection of the saints when Jesus comes back with them to lead the battle at Armageddon and to establish His Kingdom.

The apostle John described himself as a *"partner in the tribulation [thlipsis] and the kingdom and the patient endurance that are in Jesus..."* (Rev. 1:9). He also wrote to the church of Smyrna regarding their tribulation of *"ten days,"* which most probably signifies a completion of time, not merely ten literal days. They are exhorted to be faithful unto death, so that they can receive the crown of life (Rev. 2:9-10).

Justin Martyr, like most other early Christians, believed that he was already going through the Tribulation during his lifetime, thinking that things could not get much worse than what they were experiencing for their faith. His name bares the evidence of his own martyrdom for Christ's sake. We must not forget that he, as well as thousands of other early Christians, suffered such tribulations and martyrdoms exactly as Jesus predicted. And down through the ages, not only Christians, but also Jews have suffered severe persecution and tribulation, perhaps the worst of these during our recent past being the Nazi Holocaust. Even the Roman Catholic Church, disgracefully representing Christ, perpetrated horrendous crimes against God's people, both Jews and genuine Christians, by means of their inquisitions and their greedy accumulation of power and wealth worldwide. It is evidence of its terrible abuse and "prostitution" of true faith, for which it will one day be punished.

4) Present Worldwide Tribulations

What seems strange nowadays to the Christians in the Western world is that we are not suffering like most Christians have in the past, or who are suffering in the rest of the world. We here have been especially blessed because we are the exception to the rule. But we should not ignore the present tribulation of thousands of our fellow brethren. Perhaps we should be helping them out in some way or other, at least be praying for them! Yet at this moment in time, sin and evil are becoming more pronounced, even in our own comfortable Western society. We are beginning to feel threatened by liberal anti-Christian sentiment as well as by extreme Islamist ideology explicitly stating that their main goal is to get rid of Judaism and Christianity. Liberalism is submitting to Islam's ideology and goal, which is to establish a global Caliphate under Sharia law, in substitution of the One and Only True God and His Holy Word. That is clearly an Antichrist agenda, whether we see a single "Man of Lawlessness" leading it or not. The spirit of the Antichrist is already in this world and is in the process of revealing himself. Where are Christians suffering nowadays? Mainly in Muslim-dominated countries, where they are not allowed to work, study or live as the rest of the population.

According to a list by Open Doors, there are 215 million Christians experiencing high levels of persecution in the countries on the World Watch List.[51] This represents 1 in every 12 Christians worldwide. The 2018 report says that in the last year, 3,066 Christians were killed, 1,252 were abducted, 1,020 were raped or sexually harassed, and 793 churches were attacked. Islamic oppression fuels persecution in 8 of the top 10 countries where there is Christian persecution.

The Christian website *World Watch Monitor* reported an increase in Christian persecution in Iran, specifically during December of 2018: "Over 100 Christians have been arrested in Iran in the past week and nearly 150 in the past month, as part of the government's

---

[51] Open Doors, *World Watch List 2018*, https://www.opendoorsusa.org/christian-persecution/ world-watch-list/ (accessed September 20, 2018).

attempt to 'warn' Christians against proselytizing over Christmas."[52] The U.S. International Religious Freedom (USCIRF) Report for 2018[53] noted that, even though the Iranian government targeted any and all religions outside of the Shiite Islam, the estimated 300,000 Christian converts and house church leaders in Iran faced increasingly harsh sentencing: many were sentenced to at least 10 years in prison for their religious activities. "During the year, government-controlled and pro-government media outlets continued to spread anti-Christian sentiment, while anti-Christian publications proliferated online and in print throughout Iran."[54] And with a government that repeatedly calls for "Death to Israel," Iran's 15,000 Jews also live under close-scrutiny.

In addition, according to the *Open Doors* website, "converts from Islam, while not legally prosecuted, face social opposition, and are often forced to lead double lives to keep their faith hidden from family and community members."[55] It was only due to the US President Trump's pressure that Turkey finally released the Christian pastor Andrew Brunson in 2019 from his unfair incarceration, but the Turkish president Erdogan's persecution of Christians has become even more emboldened.

What possibly prevents the Muslims from becoming a unified entity are the jealousies between them, mainly between Shiite and

---

[52] World Watch Monitor, *Iran: Staggering Number of Christians Arrested – 114 in a Week*, https://www. worldwatch monitor.org/2018/12/iran-staggering-number-of-christians-arrested-114-in-a-week/ (accessed December 5, 2018).

[53] United States Commission on International Religious Freedom, *US International Religious Freedom Report*, 47, https://www.uscirf.gov/reports-briefs/annual-report/2018-annual-report (accessed December 15, 2018).

[54] Ibid, 48.

[55] Open Doors, *World Watch List 2018*, https://www.opendoorsusa.org/christian-persecution/ world-watch-list/turkey/ (accessed December 20, 2018).

Sunni. But we can quite certainly identify the "Beast from the Bottomless Pit" in general terms as this Islamic religious-political entity, and Muhammad as the "False Prophet." Even though we cannot accuse all Muslims of being evil, and we should certainly show the love of Christ to them, its ideology reflects Satan's intention of destroying Christianity, Judaism, and anything else that opposes Islam. I believe that sooner or later, the leader of an Islamist movement will start to take control, perhaps being joined by the global political power of the United Nations, the European Union, and the Vatican. It is more probable that a coalition of leaders will unite, since history proves that the world is too large for a single leader to control all by himself.

Turkey's dictator Recep Tayyip Erdogan has already announced his plans to join forces with Iran against Washington,[56] so he envisions that Turkey and Iran may sometime join sides to form a powerful united global government. In December of 2018, following the U.S. withdrawal from Syria, *The Clarion Project*,[57] said that "in addition to enabling Iranian and Russian power in the region, the U.S. withdrawal from Syria will bring Erdogan one step closer to realizing his dream of being crowned the caliph of his newly-revived neo-Ottoman empire." This is not mere speculation. Erdogan is deadly serious and announced on September 4, 2019 that he is already developing his own nuclear arms, just as Iran is doing. *Gatestone Institute* quotes his speech: "They say we can't have nuclear-tipped

---

[56] Gatestone Institute, *Turkey Turns on America*, https://www.gatestoneinstitute. org/13470/ turkey-turns- on-america (accessed December 24, 2018).

[57] Clarion Project, *How to Make Sense of US Withdrawal from Syria*, https:// clarionproject.org /how-to-make-sense-of-u-s-withdrawal-from-syria/ (accessed December 20, 2018).

missiles, though some have them. This, I can't accept."[58] Since the 1960s, United States had been storing nuclear warheads at Turkey's main four airbases as part of their NATO agreement, though after the Cold War, only a few have remained in Incirlik. But who is to stop Erdogan from ignoring its part in the Nuclear Non-proliferation Treaty made in 1980 and confiscate these for himself?

The world is presently focused on Iran, but may be blindsided by Turkey. After a failed coup in July 2016, President Erdogan took advantage of the political instability to justify his persecution of Christians and his Turkish opposition, which he is still actively pursuing. According to the well-recognized *Jerusalem Center for Public Affairs* (JCPA), Turkey has been assisting militant groups, such as the Muslim Brotherhood and other radical organizations, in many countries of the Middle East while also promoting its world dominance "as part of the revival of the Ottoman Empire legacy."[59] "Turkey's covert activities fit into its broader policy of acting as a significant actor in the Middle East...This is a Turkey headed by the militant President Erdogan who is trying to revive the Ottoman heritage and reconstitute wherever possible the unimplemented 'National Pact' of 1923...which expands Turkey's borders well beyond what is considered today to be an integral part of Syria and Iraq and of its northern and western neighbors. The latest signing of a defense agreement with Qatar allowing Turkey to deploy more than 4,000 troops in the Gulf princedom, the recent acquisition of Suakin Island off the coast of Sudan (which used to be the headquarters of the

---

[58] Gatestone Institute, *Next for Turkey? Nuclear Weapons!*, https://www.gatestoneinstitute.org/14896/ turkey-erdogan-nuclear-weapons (accessed September 18, 2019).

[59] Jerusalem Center for Public Affairs, *Turkey's Expansionist Policy Exposed*, http://jcpa.org/ turkeys-expansionist-policy-exposed/ (accessed January 30, 2019).

Ottoman fleet in the Red Sea), the military presence in Somalia and parts of Northern Iraq, assistance to Hamas in Gaza, and political activities in Jerusalem are all but different expressions of this expansionist policy, which has not met any opposition from the Arab consensus or by Iran and Russia."[60] Thus, we can see how the world events are shifting to promote a much larger Muslim Empire than there was ever in the past, even greater than the old Ottoman Empire. Though Iran seems to be a greater threat to Christians and Jews at this time, Turkey could gain much greater strength and represent a more global threat to God's people.

Nevertheless, a Rasmussen Report reflects that many in United States do not understand what is going on. A report published on February 7, 2017[61] points out that "most voters agree that Christians living in Muslim-majority countries are mistreated for their religion. But Democrats are "more likely to think Muslims are mistreated in *America* than to think Christians are persecuted in the Islamic world." And because many in the United States live in denial and prefer to defend Muslims rather than Christians, this attitude provides ample opportunity for Muslims to spread their Anti-Christian doctrine so much easier.

In the midst of this growing pro-Muslim and anti-Christian (plus anti-Jewish) sentiment worldwide, we can understand what George Ladd stated: "The final persecution of God's people by Antichrist is nothing but the consummation of the same hostility which the world and the prince of evil have manifested against God and His people throughout the entire course of the age…Believers have been ready,

---

[60] Ibid.

[61] Rasmussen Reports, http://www.rasmussenreports.com/public_content/ politics/general _politics/february_2017/democrats_think_muslims_worse_off_ here_than_christians_are_in_muslim_world (accessed September 20, 2018).

often glad, to die for Christ's sake. Why should it be any different at the end?"[62] God promised to preserve them in it, not from it. Martyrdom has always been a mark of faithfulness to God, whether Jew or Christian.

B. Daniel's Final Week

It is also essential to redefine Daniel's final 70th week. The last "week" of the 70 "weeks" in Daniel 9, interpreted by many as seven literal years, has caused great confusion and argument among theologians and everyday believers for centuries. Daniel received this specific message from God probably around the year 541 BC, the first year of King Darius the Mede (possibly the same historical figure of Cyaxares of Media, who controlled the empire for two years until Cyrus II took over in 539 BC). Daniel might have already been in Babylon for about 64 years following his captivity, so he could have been near 82 years old by then, if he was captured at the age of 18. Daniel understood that the exile and the *"desolations of Jerusalem"* would last around 70 years (Dan. 9:2; Jer. 25:1-12), and was interceding for the sins of Israel and asking God to confirm whether the time of the captivity in Babylon was nearing its end:

> *"In the first year of his reign, I, Daniel, perceived in the books the number of years that, according to the word of the LORD to Jeremiah the prophet, must pass before the end of the desolations of Jerusalem, namely, seventy years"* (Dan. 9:2).

Here Daniel interprets Jeremiah's reference to seventy years as the *"number of years that…must pass before the end of the desolations of*

---

[62] Ladd, *The Blessed Hope*, 129.

Jerusalem." It doesn't say here "at exactly" seventy years, but that seventy years must **pass** before God would start bringing the Jews back to their land.

Daniel could have estimated that the exile had begun with his own captivity in 605 BC, or maybe four years previously in 609 BC, at the death of King Josiah. He might have also used the dates of at least three general deportations after his own: between 599-598 BC, or 587-586 BC (when the Temple was destroyed), or even 581 BC, which would push the date of the return further down the line. On the other end of the time spectrum, the Persian King Cyrus II emitted the edict for the Jews to return to Israel in 539 BC, but the return was also made in three distinct stages, beginning with a group under Zerubbabel and Joshua in 538 BC, another under Ezra around 458 BC, and then another under Nehemiah around 445 BC. Evidently, the 70 years are merely an estimated lapse of time and not a clearly defined period.

In any case, after an intense period of fasting and praying, Daniel received a message through the angel Gabriel describing some events that would take place leading up to the final end of days, including the coming of the Messiah (both comings), more wars and desolations, and finally the establishment of His Kingdom. God again used the number "70" and the word "desolations," though in this case He used the representative term "weeks" instead of "years," referring to the timing:

> *"Seventy weeks are decreed about your people and your holy city, to finish the transgression, to put an end to sin, and to atone for iniquity, to bring in everlasting righteousness, to seal both vision and prophet, and to anoint a most holy place"* (Dan. 9:24, ESV).

There are many similarities between the first dispersion (around 586 BC) and the second dispersion (AD 70), but I believe that the mention of seventy in both cases is merely symbolic. God needed to teach His people a lesson about their being faithful to Him in the midst of a sinful world during Daniel's life, and it is the same lesson that He wanted to teach His people in the 1st century. Their perfection was and is still His aim, and the human time that this would require is in God's hands. A thousand years for us can be a blink of an eye for God. It will take as long as it needs, but God has determined to get the results He seeks. In the latter dispersion, it will all depend on how Israel responds to God's purposes and callings, not on a literal timeframe, and that is what we have been seeing for the past almost 2,000 years.

Even though Jesus' death around AD 33 **did** make atonement for iniquity, we cannot say that all transgression has fully ceased nor has sin totally ended. Everlasting righteousness has also not been brought in, since all these things can only occur when the Messiah is finally on His throne. So, the fulfillment of most of the above objectives still lies in the future. This would be the ultimate fullness which is implied in the "70 weeks." Note that in the Hebrew script of "70 weeks" (שבעים שבעים), both words are written the same, though pronounced *shavuim shiviim*, which seems like it is more about its spiritual significance than about a literal period. Many times, in the Hebrew Bible we find a play on words that has a more hidden significance than at first glance. The root word is *sheva*, as also the root for *Shabbat*, which seems to imply that God will obtain total rest for mankind after accomplishing His eternal purposes with them.

Since different translators can reflect their personal perspectives,

I would like to look at Jay P. Green's *The Interlinear Bible*[63], which translates the last part of verse 24 literally as: *"…and to anoint the Most Holy."* The original Hebrew text is transliterated as: *"L'mashach kadosh kadoshim,"* which means "to anoint the holy of holies," very possibly referring to the Messiah Himself, because the Old Testament term for the Holy of Holies in the Tabernacle always has the article *"ha"* (for "the") before *"kadoshim,"* as in *kadosh hakadoshim*. Here it refers to the Most Holy One.

Regarding the timing, verse 25 clarifies something specific about the first 69 weeks, or "7 weeks and 62 weeks" needed for fulfilling the first part of the prophecy in verse 24: *"Know, then, and understand that from the going out of a word to restore and to rebuild Jerusalem, to Messiah the Prince, shall be seven weeks and sixty-two weeks"* (Green's Interlinear Bible). Verse 25 talks about the city streets and walls being rebuilt in difficult times during the first 7 weeks, and then verse 26a adds: *"And after 62 weeks, Messiah will be cut off, but not (of) Himself"* (Green's Interlinear Bible). Some people interpret that this refers to the arrival of the Messiah at His birth, but the last part of the verse clarifies that it refers to His death.

Cyrus gave the word for rebuilding Jerusalem around 539 BC, and around AD 33 the Messiah was killed for our transgressions. We can safely assume that, even though He was killed by the Romans, this was also done with God's permission. Should we really try to count the exact days of this period? Some have proposed a formula for producing a precise "69 weeks" from start to finish, interpreting each week as 7 years rather than 7 days, and taking into account the Hebrew calendar year of 360 days, plus a "correction" regarding the year zero and when Jesus was actually born. If we want to produce

---

[63] Jay P. Green, *The Interlinear Bible, Hebrew-Greek-English*, 2nd ed. (Peabody, Mass.: Hendrickson, 1986), 691.

a literal time period of 69 "weeks of years" or 483 years for the fulfillment of Daniel 9:25-26a, we must start counting the years at 539 BC, when Cyrus put out the decree to rebuild Jerusalem. If we add 33 years to that (Jesus' estimated year of death when He was "cut off"), it adds up to a total 572 years, rather than 483. Some finish counting the 69 weeks at the time when Jesus began His ministry rather than at His death. Even if we do all the adjustments in order to produce a neat 483 years using some preferred starting and finishing point, the exact days and weeks are not the important part of this prophecy. They are probably just meant to reflect a series of chronological events from start to finish, time that could be lengthened or shortened by mankind's actions or inactions, or by God's own calendar, which is outside of our human understanding.

Eusebius of Caesarea, of the 3rd century, wrote a series of theological documents titled *Demostratio Evangelica*[64] (Proof of the Gospel). Regarding the seventy weeks of Daniel, he proposed the following:

> "The whole period of our Saviour's Teaching and working of Miracles is said to have been **three-and-a-half years**, which is half a week…One week of years therefore would be represented by the whole period of His association with the Apostles, both the time before His Passion, and the time after His Resurrection…But after His Resurrection He was most likely with His disciples a period equal to the

---

[64] Eusebius, *Demostratio Evangelica*, Book VIII, Ch. 2, 137-138, trans. W. J. Ferrar, IntraText Edition, Society for Promoting Christian Knowledge (London: The Macmillan Company, 1920), http://www.intratext.com/IXT/ENG0882/_P38.HTM (accessed September 20, 2018).

years, being seen of them **forty days**,…as the Acts of the Apostles tells us. So that this would be the prophet's week of years, during which He "**confirmed a covenant with many**," confirming that is to say the **new Covenant** of the Gospel Preaching. And who were the many to whom He confirmed it, but His own **disciples and Apostles**, and such of the **Hebrews who believed** in Him? And moreover, half through this week, during which He confirmed the said Covenant with many, the sacrifice and libation was taken away, and the **abomination of desolation began**, for in the middle of this week after the three-and-a-half days of His Teaching, at the time when He suffered, the Veil of the Temple was torn asunder from the top to the bottom, so that in effect from that time **sacrifice and libation were taken away**, and the abomination of desolation stood in the holy place, inasmuch as **the Being had left them desolate**…And from that time a succession of all kinds of **troubles** afflicted the whole nation and their city until the last war against them, and the final siege, in which **destruction rushed on them like a flood** with all kinds of misery of famine, plague and sword, and all who had conspired against the Saviour in their youth were cut off; then, too, the abomination of desolation stood in the Temple, and it has remained there even till to-day, while they have daily reached deeper depths of desolation. And perhaps this will be so until the end of the world, according to the limit set by the prophet when he said, 'And unto the consummation of time a fulfilment shall be given to the **desolation**.'"

We see here many uncommon ways of interpreting this text, some of which I agree with and others that I don't agree with. Eusebius reflects the same problem that many have today in thinking that Daniel's apocalyptic last week should be understood in a literal way. He associated Jesus' 3½ years of ministry as the first segment of the 3½ years in Revelation, which Midtribulationists modernly identify as the duration of the saints' tribulation before the "rapture." Eusebius then creatively applied the other half of the seven years to the forty days of Jesus being with His disciples. This clearly makes no sense. Yet he identified God as the "One" who would confirm a Covenant with many, which is the way I see it. God is also the One who put an end to the Jewish sacrifices and offerings in the Temple, though Eusebius believed that the abomination of desolation appeared at the same time when Christ died, after which began the time of desolations.

Most theologians agree that the Messiah the "Prince" in verse 25, is not the same as the destroying "prince" in verse 26: "...*And the people of the prince who is to come shall destroy the city and the sanctuary...*" (Dan. 9:26, ESV). Nevertheless, I believe that after the "anointed one" or Messiah was "cut off," the last symbolic "week" of Daniel was **initiated** rather than **interrupted**. Pretribulationists allege that this is when the "eschatological clock" stopped.

The last part of verse 26 in Green's Interlinear Bible says: "...*And the end shall be with the flood, and ruins are determined, until the end shall be war.*" This clearly implies a long time-span, but we can most assuredly state that the prediction in verse 26 about the destruction of the city and sanctuary was fulfilled in AD 70, when Jerusalem and the Temple were destroyed for a second time, in this instance by Rome. Green translates "desolations" as "ruins," referring to what Jerusalem experienced after AD 70, which I believe includes the "abomination of desolations" that was placed on the Temple Mount by the Muslims six centuries later, and which still remains to this day.

The following verse 27 is quite controversial due to the difficulty in the Hebrew wording, which can be understood in various ways. The ESV version says:

> *"And he shall make a strong covenant with many for one week, and for half of the week he shall put an end to sacrifice and offering. And on the wing of abominations shall come one who makes desolate, until the decreed end is poured out on the desolator"* (Dan. 9:27, ESV).

We can analyze this verse easier by dividing it into four segments according to Green's Interlinear Bible, emphasizing the corresponding subjects in each one:

- *"And **he** shall confirm a covenant with the many for one week"* (27a).
- *"And in the middle of the week **he** shall cause the sacrifice and the offering to cease"* (27b).
- *"And on a corner **[there will be]** desolating abominations, even until the end"* (27c).
- *"And that which was decreed shall pour out on **the desolator"** (27d).

Regarding 27a, the Hebrew text does not describe who this "he" is. Nowadays, most people believe that it refers to the Antichrist and the "covenant" that he will allegedly make with the Jewish people because the Hebrew term *"higbir"* can imply a powerful violent action.

Nevertheless, *higbir* simply means to confirm or make something solid and unchanging, like Green's translation describes as he *"shall confirm a covenant."* Pretribulationists propose that the Jews will rebuild the Temple, which the Antichrist will then destroy in the middle of those seven years. This is totally preposterous, given the extreme sensitivity of Muslims when they feel even a minimum amount of threat to their Mosque on the Temple Mount. Some can't deny that problem, so they propose that both the Mosque and the Temple will exist side by side, which is also clearly impossible. It makes much more Biblical and logical sense to understand that this "person" is **God** through **His Messiah Jesus**, who declared He was going to make the **New Covenant** with **"the many."** As stated before, I believe that we are already, and still presently, going through Daniel's "last week" in an extended sense, which began when the New Covenant was made with "the many" and will not end until Jesus returns as King at the start of the Millennium.

Below are important Bible verses that use the term "many" in reference to believers that were included in the powerful New Covenant:

> *"Therefore I will divide him a portion with **the many**, and he shall divide the spoil with the strong, because he poured out his soul to death and was numbered with the transgressors; yet he bore the sin of many, and makes intercession for the transgressors"* (Isa. 53:12).

> *"…even as the Son of Man came not to be served but to serve, and to give his life as a ransom **for many**"* (Matt. 20:28 and Mk. 10:45).

*"…for this is my blood of the covenant, which is poured out **for many** for the forgiveness of sins"* (Matt. 26:28).

*"…For if many died through one man's trespass [Adam's], much more have the grace of God and the free gift by the grace of that one man Jesus Christ abounded **for many**"* (Rom. 5:15).

*"…so Christ, having been offered once to bear the sins **of many**, will appear a second time, not to deal with sin but to save those who are eagerly waiting for him"* (Heb. 9:28).

Why was there such an emphasis on the word "many" in reference to Jesus' atoning death? It seems like it really is in reference to Daniel 9:27. It doesn't seem to be purely coincidental. Also, what does 27b add about the "one" in 27a who will make a Covenant with the many for "a week," which could simply imply a perfect period-of-time? *"He will put an end to sacrifice and offering."* **God** ultimately allowed this to happen in AD 70 by means of the Roman rulers. It was God who caused the sacrifice to cease, because Jesus was the perfect and ultimate sacrifice for our sin as mediator of the New Covenant (Heb. 9:12-15). He made sure that Israel would never again make sacrifices and offerings, though it took about 27 more years after Jesus' death in order for the Temple to be destroyed. It was not fulfilled immediately.

Regarding the tricky question of the timing in 27b, Green's Interlinear Bible says: *"And in the middle of the week he shall cause the sacrifice and the offering to cease…"* (27b). There can be a variety of interpretations for this. The Hebrew transliteration simply says: *"ve jetzi ha shavúa…,"* which could mean *"in the midst"* or *"in the middle"* of the week, and not necessarily *"for half a week,"* as the ESV states. This could make a lot of difference if one does not try to force this to signify 3½ literal years. It could just imply that God would cause the sacrifices to cease at some time during that extended period, which He already did. Even though Jamieson, Fausset, and Brown were Pretribulationists in their outlook and believed that God had finished His relationship with the Jews until it would be renewed in the Kingdom, they wrote that the "One" who confirmed the covenant was **Jesus**. They added:

> "The confirmation of the covenant is assigned to Him [Jesus] also else-where. Isaiah 42:6, 'I will give thee for a covenant of the people' (that is, He in whom the covenant between Israel and God is personally expressed)."[65]

Jamieson, Fausset, and Brown also believed that **the Messiah** was the One to cause all sacrifices to "utterly" cease (Daniel 8:11; 11:31). Nevertheless, they stated that "Israel reached the summit of abominations, which drew down desolation," thus interpreting that the "desolations" refers to **Israel's apostasy**, rather than to something forced upon them by a **foreign government**.[66]

These authors also referred that Isaac Newton believed that the Covenant was confirmed when Jesus died, 3½ years after beginning His ministry, and then the Temple was destroyed after 3½ years, between spring of AD 67 and autumn AD 70.[67] But this would require a break in time of about 30 years between the first event and the second. Then Jamieson, Fausset, and Brown quoted Francis Bacon (in *Advancement of Learning* 2:3), who said:

---

[65] Jamieson, Fausset, and Brown, *One Volume Commentary* (Grand Rapids, MI: Associated Publishers and Authors, 1871, republished no date), 641.

[66] Ibid, 642.

[67] Ibid.

"Prophecies are of the nature of the Author, with whom **a thousand years are as one day**; and therefore, are not fulfilled punctually at once, but have a **springtime and germinant accomplishment through many years**, though the height and fullness of them may refer to one age."[68]

Evidently, Bacon visualized a less literal calendar for the fulfillment of Daniel's "last week," which could extend for many, many years "since a thousand years are as one day," perhaps better conceived as "one age."

J. Barton Payne agreed that the subject in 9:27a and 27b refers to the **Messiah**, who proclaimed the Gospel for 3½ years and confirmed the "grace of the divine testament," but which also "brought to a close the OT economy of redemption." This caused all sacrifice to cease, and then for the last 3½ years, the covenant continued to be confirmed with Israel up to the time of the stoning of Stephen and the Church's expulsion from Jerusalem.[69] But this implies that the seven years of Daniel have already finished, which they evidently have not, since not all the elements of Daniel 9:24 have been fulfilled.

On the other hand, it is presumptuous to think that the "he" in sections 27a and 27b refers to the Antichrist merely because those phrases are found right before 27c. The two previous phrases do not have to be speaking about the same person mentioned in the third phrase. The ancient Hebrew Bible texts did not have a period between each sentence, nor did they have capital letters, nor were the

---

[68] Ibid.

[69] Payne, J. B., *Encyclopedia of Biblical Prophecy* (New York: Harper & Row, 1973), 388.

verses numbered. That is why the word *"and"* in the Hebrew text is so very important: *"And on the wing of abominations shall come **one** who makes desolate…"*, though Green's translation reads: *"And on a corner [**there will be**] desolating abominations…"*

This can now easily refer to something or someone different than in the previous segments. Actually, the noun in 27c is only implied, indicating that it does not have to refer to a person, but can easily refer to the Muslim mosque that was set up there many centuries ago. Islam established its abomination on the Temple Mount and will perpetuate desolations until the end-times.

There are also questions about the "corner" or "wing" in verse 27c. A transliteration of that part in the Hebrew text says: *"ve al kanaf shikutzim meshamen,"* which literally means: "and **on a wing or corner**, abominations will cause desolations." This could simply refer to an area on the Temple Mount. And what do we see on a section of the Temple Mount at this moment? Ever since the 7th century, the Muslim mosque has caused and perpetuated the desolations.

This evokes the much-disputed discussion about 2 Thessalonians 2:4, which describes the "Man of Lawlessness" as one who will take his seat in the "temple of God." But grammatically, the Greek term *naon tou Theu* for "God's temple" could mean any kind of sanctuary or sacred space, whether Jewish, Christian, Muslim, or anything else. The text does not say that it will be a strictly Jewish Temple. Ask a Muslim what is on the Temple Mount today, and he will clearly say that it is Allah's Noble Sanctuary, and that Allah is the true God. For them, this "god" has supplanted the real God of Israel. It could also imply that no one has to rebuild the Temple for the Antichrist when he is to appear and claim it for himself because it already belongs to his religious system. This future "Man of Lawlessness," which I believe will be a Muslim leader, could easily sit upon God's sanctuary or sacred space because the Muslims already possess it and are still trampling it.

The rest of section 27c describes how long these desolations will last: *"…even until the end."* This implies that the Muslim mosque will still be standing there until the coming of the Messiah. Admittedly, if anyone tries to destroy it, it will create another world war. It has to remain there until the return of the Messiah, who will destroy it with the breath of His coming (2 Thess. 2:8). The section 27d adds (Green's version): *"And that which was decreed shall pour out on the desolator."* Jesus will destroy this *naon* (sanctuary) of the Antichrist and then build the Third Temple when He returns. Only Jesus can destroy it, and only Jesus can rebuild it unto God, and the timing is totally in God's control.

C. God's Two Witnesses

1) The two anointed ones: Israel and the Church

One of the first verses that stood out to my attention, as I began to study the events of the end-times, was Zechariah 4. This is a clear reference to God's two witnesses in all the earth. The prophet Zechariah said:

> *"I see, and behold, a lampstand all of gold, with a bowl on the top of it, and seven lamps on it, with seven lips on each of the lamps that are on the top of it. And there are **two olive trees** by it, one on the right of the bowl and the other on its left"* (Zech. 4:2).

Zechariah then asked the angel: *"What are these two branches of the olive trees, which are beside the two golden pipes from which the golden oil is poured out?"* (Zech. 4:12). The angel's answer was: *"These are the **two anointed ones** who **stand by the Lord** of the whole earth"* (Zech. 4:14).

The angel does not clarify who these two anointed ones are, but they could easily be a symbol of two people groups rather than two literal individuals. God told Moses to stand by Him, so that he would hear God's commandments and then teach them to the Israelites: *"But you, **stand here by me**, and I will tell you the whole commandment and the statutes and the rules that you shall teach them, that they may do them in the land that I am giving them to possess"* (Deut. 5:31). In a very similar manner, Jesus told Paul regarding the Gospel: *"But rise and **stand upon your feet**, for I have appeared to you for this purpose, to appoint you as a servant and witness to the things in which you have seen me and to those in which I will appear to you…"* (Acts 26:16). This may imply that both the Old Testament and the New Testament faithful people are God's witnesses unto the nations.

If we study other verses in the same and previous chapter of Zechariah, we can also make an association between Zerubbabel and Israel, and between Joshua and the Church. Even though historically Zerubbabel was the one who rebuilt the Second Temple after the Jews began to return to the Land from Babylon, he can also be seen to represent all of Israel when the Messiah comes forth from it: *"Who are you, O great mountain? Before Zerubbabel you shall become a plain. And he shall **bring forward the top stone** amid shouts of 'Grace, grace to it!'"* (Zech. 4:7). This "top stone" can be understood to be Jesus, the chief cornerstone (Eph. 2:20), who was brought forth from Israel as God's grace to humanity.

Regarding Joshua, God cleansed him from his iniquity and gave him clean garments so as to minister and intercede for God's people

(Zech. 3:4). Joshua was dressed in the garments of a high priest and was told: *"If you will walk in my ways and keep my charge, then you shall* **rule my house** *and have charge of my courts, and I will give you the* **right of access** *among those who are standing here"* (Zech. 3:7). Christians have also been given this charge of walking in God's ways, plus the responsibility to rule in His Kingdom among those previously walking in God's ways, namely Israel. The following verse contains several elements that could also compare Joshua to Christians. He is to be a **sign** and witness of the "**Branch**," who removed the iniquity of the land in one day, whose name is engraved on a single stone with seven eyes.

> *"Hear now, O Joshua the high priest, you and your friends who sit before you, for they are men who are* **a sign***: behold, I will bring* **my servant the Branch***. For behold, on the stone that I have set before Joshua, on a single stone with seven eyes, I will engrave its inscription, declares the LORD of hosts, and* **I will remove the iniquity of this land in a single day***"* (Zech. 3:8-9).

Even Joshua's name, in Hebrew script, is the same as Jesus' name, which means "salvation." Thus, following proper exegetical hermeneutics, these *"two anointed ones who stand by the Lord of the whole earth"* (Zech. 4:14) can represent both **Israel** and the **Church.**

In the same manner, the reference in Revelation 11 to two "witnesses" also corresponds to Israel and the Church: *"These are the* **two olive trees** *and the* **two lampstands** *that* **stand before the Lord** *of the earth"* (Rev. 11:4). They would originally have had God's authority to testify to the nations about His ways. They would prophesy, stop the rain from falling, turn the waters into blood and strike the earth with plagues by God's power (Rev. 11:6). The Holy

Spirit definitely manifested that power through the early nation of Israel, and then through the early Church. Their being dressed in sackcloth refers to their piety and faithfulness to God. We read that both witnesses would preach of God's truth, whether the Law or the Gospel, for 1,260 days (Rev. 11:3). This can be related to Revelation 12 where we see that Christians, at first, would conquer Satan by *"the blood of the Lamb and by the word of their testimony"* (Rev. 12:11). When the dragon (Satan) pursued Israel, she was "nourished" by God in the wilderness for a symbolic time of 3½ years, during which time Christians also began to be persecuted by the same dragon. Thus, at some point in the "middle" of the symbolic seven years, things changed and they lost their power.

This can also be associated with the prophecy in Daniel about a "horn" that would come up from the fourth beast to *"make war with the saints and prevail over them"* (Dan. 7:21). These three mentions of tribulation and persecution against God's people in Daniel 7, Revelation 11, and Revelation 12 seem to be parallel, when an evil leader or government would temporarily triumph over the saints. What can confuse the issue of these witnesses in Revelation 11 is the description of their supposed "deaths," as seen in the statement: *"And when they have finished their testimony, the beast that rises from the bottomless pit will **make war** on them and **conquer** them and **kill** them…"* (Rev. 11:7). This is just another way of saying what Daniel described as: *"…this horn made war with the saints and prevailed over them"* (Dan. 7:21). If we interpret Revelation 11:7 literally, the two witnesses would only preach during the first half of the "seven years" and then they would lie dead and rotting in the street of Jerusalem for the second half. As stated before, I do not believe in constraining the "seven years" to natural days or years, but see them as an extended figurative time. As evidenced by history, the message of both witnesses was initially accompanied by signs of great divine power, but later on, Satan managed to suppress this miraculous power and authority, and effectively "kill" them.

We must honestly admit that neither the modern Israel nor the modern Church possess the same power as what is described in our Bible texts. What has changed? Some modernly allege that God only extended His mighty hand during those early Israelite and Christian times so that the miracles could be recorded in our Scriptures. This seems to be a simple justification of what is evidently lacking among God's modern people, both Christians and Jews. Israel was dispersed among the nations of the world while the "Church" was destroyed by the pride and carnality imbued in it by Satan. This can be seen in the downfall of the Christian Byzantine Empire, the "prostitution" of the Roman Catholic Church and the persecution of true believers later on. Could this be the spiritual "death" of Israel and the Church described in the middle of the extended period of "tribulation"? Even today, it seems like Satan has so destroyed or influenced God's people spiritually that there is very little faith left in His miraculous power as before.

2) Jews and Christians raised out of their tribulations

As said before, the time-lapse between Daniel's already fulfilled 69 years and the beginning of the 70th year is illustrated by Pretribulationists as a "pause in God's timeclock." But we must remember that to God, one day is the same as a thousand years, and a thousand years as one day (2 Pet. 3:8). God simply does not stop working. On the other hand, the Pretribulational premise that the last week of Daniel needs to be fulfilled literally because the first 69 weeks were fulfilled literally is a very weak argument. Even if this were true (which is debatable), it is not solid enough proof of the need that this last "week" be fulfilled in the same manner. I believe that we should stop worrying about how the numbers may or may not add up. Rather, we should be satisfied that Daniel's prophecies will be fulfilled within God's perfect timeframe and not according to our imperfect human timeframe.

The important thing is that God's witnesses will be raised **from in midst of their tribulation**. These are the ones who will be raised from the dead when God gives them the command to rise: ***"Come up!"*** (Rev. 11:12), those who *"…have washed their robes and made them white in the blood of the Lamb"* (Rev. 7:14). God initially told the Jewish people that they will be raised from in midst of their tribulation, as Psalm 50:15 says: *"and call upon me **in the day of trouble**; I will **deliver** you, and you shall glorify me."* He also said about the timing: *"Alas! That day is so great there is none like it; it is a time of distress for Jacob; yet he shall be **saved out of it**"* (Jer. 30:7). This clearly says "out of it" while in the day of trouble, not "from it," referring to the resurrection at the end of their tribulation. And God told the same thing to the Christians, which would be *"immediately **after the tribulation of those days**"* (Matt. 24:29-30).

D. The Antichrist

1) Various Historical Evil Kingdoms

There have been many evil empires and rulers in this world during mankind's existence, but very few are mentioned in the Bible. We only read about those that have something to do with the territorial area around Israel, mostly in the Middle East, or around the Mediterranean Sea. The main purpose of mentioning these nations in Scripture is to describe how they affect God's relationship with Israel. He has mostly focused on the areas not much further than Lebanon and Assyria (to the north), Edom, Babylon, and Persia (to the East), Greece and Rome (to the West), and Egypt, Arabia and Ethiopia (to the south). There is a mention of Russia when describing the war of Gog and Magog in Ezekiel 38-39, which I place *"in the latter years,"* at the end of the Millennium. Only at that time will Israel *"dwell securely,"* but the end will be brought about by God Himself. (To be discussed in more detail later.) Most of the rest of the world is just described generically as nations, coastlands, and islands.

Thus, the first four empires that repeatedly stand out in the prophecies of Daniel are the Babylonian, Median/Persian, Greek, and Roman empires. All these nations impacted ancient Israel in negative ways, causing great tribulation for God's people, including the destruction of both Temples and their following dispersions, first to Babylon and then to all the world. Nevertheless, God allowed this to happen in order to perfect Israel for His glory. I believe that other later enemies in the same region are indirectly hinted at in Biblical prophecy, including the early Muslim-Arab conquests and the Muslim Ottoman Empire in the formerly Assyrian territories. These can be seen as fulfilling many prophesies regarding the tribulation and persecution against God's people, both Jews and Christians, in our more recent history.

2) **Many antichrists and false prophets**

Let us look at the prophecies often used to describe the future "Antichrist." We must first analyze whether any of those have already had a historic fulfillment, and then study those that could refer to someone or something still our future. Three crucial topics that were mentioned repeatedly in Daniel's prophecies are: the death of the "Anointed" or Messiah; the destruction of God's Temple in Jerusalem along with the removal of regular burnt offerings; and the establishment of the abomination of desolations on the Temple Mount (Dan. 8:10-13, 25; 9:25-26; 11:31; 12:11). Looking back in history, we know that the Messiah was crucified sometime around AD 33; the Second Temple was destroyed by the Roman Empire in AD 70; and the abomination of desolations was established upon the Temple Mount around AD 691 by the Muslims (though they had already taken it over around AD 637). Whenever these events are mentioned in any prophecy, we must not try to interpret them as belonging to our future since they have already been fulfilled as predicted.

Regarding the term "Antichrist," it is only used in 1 and 2 John as a general term for all people who oppose Jesus the Messiah with an antichrist spirit, though it could also refer to a specific future evil leader that is coming (1 Jn. 2:18). But there have been, and will be, many antichrists or deceivers in the world. Anyone who denies the Father and the Son is the antichrist (1 Jn. 2:22), and those who do not confess that Jesus is from God has the spirit of the antichrist (1 Jn. 4:3).

Clearly, history has had its share of antichrists (2 Jn. 1:7), but we must be careful when we try to identify the worldwide dictator of the final days. Jesus spoke about many false Christs and false prophets (also antichrists) that would arise to lead astray His elect, if possible. Taking advantage of the expectancy of Jesus' return, many could perform great signs and wonders, and some may say: "Look, here is the Christ!" or "Look, there he is!" Jesus warned us not to believe them. Not even Jesus knew exactly when He would come back, since He said that this is totally in the Father's hands (Matt. 24:36; Mk. 13:32). On the other hand, maybe there won't even be a single "Antichrist," but an antichrist governing coalition.

As stated before, Satan has been persecuting the Church for centuries, at the same time in which Israel was persecuted and dispersed throughout the world without a land up to 1948, when the nation of Israel was finally rebirthed. This dispersion or "great tribulation" in accordance with **Revelation 12** is evidently just a representative extension of time, way beyond the literal 1,260 days or 3½ years.

> *"But the woman was given the two wings of the great eagle so that she might fly from the serpent into the wilderness, to the place where she is to be nourished for **a time, and times, and half a time**…Then the dragon became furious with the woman and went off to make war on the rest of her offspring, on those who keep the commandments of God and hold to the testimony of Jesus…"* (Rev. 12:14-15, 16-17).

Early in that time, God gave the Church the power to conquer the serpent/dragon by the blood of the Lamb and the word of their testimony, but some would also be called to give their lives for God's commandments and the testimony of Jesus.

3) **Beasts and Horns**

When apocalyptic texts speak about a "beast," it is almost always in reference to a government, empire, or the leader of an empire. We find several "horns" described in the visions of Daniel, which also represent various empires and their leaders. We will begin with Daniel 8, where the angel Gabriel mentioned two beasts and explained who they were in verses 20-21: the **ram** represents the empire of Media and Persia, and the **goat** represents the empire of Greece.

"Then the goat became exceedingly great [Greece], *but when he was strong, the **great horn** [probably referring to Alexander the Great] was broken, and instead of it there came up **four conspicuous horns** toward the four winds of heaven"* (Dan. 8:8).

The four horns that came up after the "great horn" was broken could easily refer to the four territorial kingdoms that arose after Alexander died in 323 BC: Ptolemaic Egypt, Seleucid Mesopotamia and Central Asia, Attalid Anatolia, and Antigonid Macedon. Seleucus established the Seleucid Empire in Babylon in 312 BC, which slowly extended from Greece to India, including Israel, until it was destroyed by nascent Rome in 63 BC. Daniel 8:9-12 continues saying:

*"Out of one of them came **a little horn** [Rome], which grew exceedingly **great** toward the south, toward the east, and toward the **glorious land** [Israel]. It grew great, even to the host of heaven. And some of the host and some of the stars it threw down to the ground and trampled on them. It **became great**, even as great as the **Prince of the host** [Jesus the Messiah]. And the **regular burnt offering was taken away** from him, and the place of his **sanctuary was overthrown** [AD 70]. And a host will be given over to it [the Jewish people] together with the regular burnt offering because of transgression, and it will throw truth to the ground, and it will act and prosper."*

Some interpret that this "little horn" refers to Antiochus IV Epiphanes, since he profaned the Temple with pagan symbols and sacrifices. But he never permanently overthrew the sanctuary, and the mention of the "little horn" that **came out of one of the four horns** evidently points to another government following the Seleucid kingdom, clearly referring to the **Roman Empire**. The further mention of the "Prince of the host" also places this "horn" at a later time because it means that Jesus had already come by then.

It is also very significant that the question arose regarding the length of time in which the Sanctuary would be trampled underfoot.

> *"Then I heard a holy one speaking, and another holy one said to the one who spoke, 'For how long is the vision concerning the regular burnt offering, the transgression that makes desolate, and the giving over of the sanctuary and host to be **trampled underfoot**?' And he said to me, 'For **2,300 evenings and mornings**. Then the sanctuary shall be restored to its rightful state'"* (Dan. 8:13).

These 2,300 days obviously represent the time that will transpire from the destruction of the Temple to when it will be rebuilt in its rightful state or condition. This evidently is not a literal time, because it has been much more than 2,300 days since then, and the Temple has not yet been rebuilt. I also understand that only the Messiah can rebuild the Temple because only **He** can build it **rightfully**, as the verse indicates, and it must only be when He comes to establish His Kingdom.

Daniel 8 then describes a Roman ruler at the end of the Seleucid kingdom, though it may not refer to just a single person. I believe that it could refer to the whole **Herodian dynasty**, the various "Herods" in the Bible, though not presented in strict chronological order:

"And at the latter end of their kingdom [the Seleucid kingdom], *when the transgressors have reached their limit, a **king of bold face*** [Herod the Great], *one who understands riddles, shall arise. His power shall be great—but **not by his own power*** [supported by Rome]*; and **he*** [Herod Agrippa I and II] *shall cause fearful destruction and shall succeed in what he does, and **destroy mighty men and the people who are the saints*** [new Christians and Jews]. *By his cunning he shall make deceit prosper under his hand, and **in his own mind he shall become great.** Without warning he shall destroy many* [Herod the Great, again]. *And **he*** [Herod Antipas] *shall even rise up **against the Prince of princes*** [Jesus], *and **he*** [Herod Agrippa I] *shall be broken—but **by no human hand"*** (Dan. 8:23-25).

Thus, I believe that the above text first refers to **Herod the Great** as the "king of bold face," who began the dynasty of several consecutive Herods that followed in his footsteps. Herod the Great tried to kill Jesus as a baby and was a cruel tyrant, even towards his own royal family. He was known for being very cunning and deceitful. **Herod Antipas** was king in Judea at the time of Jesus' crucifixion and participated in His death, mentioned as the **Prince of princes**, and then **Herod Agrippa I** began to persecute and kill the new Christian believers. Acts 12:1 says that Herod Agrippa I killed James, the brother of John, and he even tried to kill Peter. Acts 12:23 says that an angel of God struck Herod Agrippa I when he accepted worship of himself instead of giving the glory to God. **Herod Agrippa II** participated in putting down the Jewish revolt in AD 70 and in destroying Jerusalem, together with Rome. Thus, I believe that the above text does not refer to a future Antichrist, because all the events described were fulfilled by the various Herodian kings.

Let us now look at Daniel 11, where we read of a "mighty king" following the kings of Persia, who is evidently Alexander the Great, whose kingdom was later divided into four.

> *"Behold, three more kings shall arise in **Persia**, and a fourth shall be far richer than all of them…Then a **mighty king** shall arise* [Alexander the Great], *who shall rule with great dominion and do as he wills… And as soon as he has arisen, **his kingdom shall be broken and divided toward the four winds of heaven**"* (Dan. 11:1-4).

We then see a long series of military deployments, describing a future king of the south [Egypt], whose daughter [Cleopatra?] will have great authority: *"…the daughter of the king of the south shall come to the king of the north to make an agreement,"* but *"she shall not retain the strength of her arm"* (Dan. 11:5-6). One from her roots shall arise, and shall import the gods of the north [Roman gods?] to Egypt (Dan. 11:8).

The kings of the north [Rome?] and the kings of the south [Egypt?] will then continue to do battle. A *"contemptible person"* from the north [Roman emperor Tiberius during the time of King Herod Antipas I?] will sweep away many armies, even the *"Prince of the Covenant,"* referring again to Jesus the Messiah: *"Armies shall be utterly swept away before him and broken, even **the prince of the covenant"*** (Dan. 11:22). Several Roman leaders will then devise plans against strongholds, but only for a time (v. 24). It was the later Emperor Vespasian who was set against the Holy Covenant [Israel], and *"forces from him shall appear and **profane the temple and fortress**, and shall **take away the regular burnt offering**…"* (Dan. 11:31a).

The above first part of Daniel 11:31 evidently refers to the Roman destruction of the Temple in AD 70, while the second half of that verse: *"...And they shall **set up the abomination that makes desolate**"* (v. 31b) was fulfilled by the later Muslim conquerors when they established their abomination on the Temple Mount about 620 years later.

We could then consider the nondescript "king" who appears in the next verses of Daniel 11:36-39 as possibly referring to **Muhammad** and the appearance of **Islam**, along with centuries of violent Muslim conquests by subsequent warriors *"with the help of a **foreign god**."* This can be related to the Beast from the Bottomless Pit in Revelation 11:7, which I also identify as Islam, a new religion spawned by Satan and spread by conquest and destruction.

> *"He* [Muhammad] *shall **exalt himself and magnify himself*** *above every god, and shall speak astonishing things against the God of gods. **He shall prosper till the indignation is accomplished***; *for what is decreed shall be done. He shall **pay no attention to the gods of his fathers*** [the ancient multi-divinity Arabian deities], *or to the one beloved by women* [Tammuz?]. *He shall not pay attention to any other god, for he shall magnify himself above all. He shall honor **the god of fortresses*** [conquest and war] *instead of these...He shall deal with the strongest fortresses **with the help of a foreign god*** [**Allah**]..." (Dan. 11:36-40).

What is of utmost importance is that this person and his foreign god *"shall prosper **till the indignation is accomplished**,"* which seems to place him as **extending into** the latter days, as the influence of Islam is proving to do so since its early inception. In the meantime, the "wise" will *"be refined, purified, and made white, **until*** *the time of the end, for it* **still awaits the appointed time**" (Dan. 11:33-35). This text implies **much tribulation** for God's people as well as the **passing of a great deal of time** before *"the indignation is accomplished,"* or *"until the time of the end,"* because *"it still awaits the appointed time."* More to my point, the mentioned "mighty king" and most others described in Daniel 11:1-39 do not refer to a future Antichrist, but just to leaders in our historic past and the birth of Islam.

Daniel 7:25 also seems to describe the early formation of Islam during a time when there will still be saints living in the world, since these will be persecuted and given into his hand. He will speak blasphemous words against God, and will think to change the times and the law. This could refer to the new Muslim calendar and the Muslim Sharia law.

> *"He shall speak words against the Most High, and shall wear out the saints of the Most High and shall* **think to change the times and the law**; *and they shall be given into his hand for* **a time, times, and half a time**" (Dan. 7:25).

On the other hand, Daniel 11:40 and onward refers to some future ruler or government that will appear **"at the time of the end."** Since Daniel 11:40-45 seems to be directly related to the previous verses that I identify as describing the appearance of Islam, this could also be a Muslim leader who will *"come into the glorious land,"* or Israel, where *"tens of thousands will fall"* (v. 41). Edom and Moab and other countries will be delivered, probably because they will join him, though Egypt will not (v. 42). He will control all the treasure and precious things of Egypt, but the Libyans and Cushites will also join him (v. 43). More importantly, he will *"pitch his palatial tents between the* *sea and the glorious holy mountain"* (Dan. 11:45). This can definitely be related to the future Antichrist, though I believe it will be after the resurrection of God's people.

Let us now turn our attention to Daniel 7, where we read about what I have termed the **"Other Little Horn"** in verse 8 (the same "other" horn in verse 20), and the **"Different Horn"** in verse 24. In this chapter we read about **four beasts that "arise from the sea"** (verse 3), as well as **four beasts that "arise from the earth"** (verse 17), both having their equivalent in the book of Revelation. These seem to be identical, yet also somewhat different. They are closely related here as well as in Revelation. There also seems to be a sequential order in regards to timing.

First of all, the first four beasts from the sea in Daniel 7 include a **lion** with eagle's wings who turned into a man, a **bear** with three ribs in its mouth, a **leopard** with four wings, and a fourth **more terrifying beast with ten horns**. The angel did not specify which kings or countries are represented by the first three beasts, though they could again refer to Babylon, Media/Persia, and Greece based on other similar visions given to the prophet Daniel (Dan. 2:37-44; 8:20-21). But the fourth beast was *"terrifying and dreadful and exceedingly strong…It was different from all the beasts that were before it, and **it had ten horns**"* (Dan. 7:7). He is later described as *"exceedingly terrifying, with its teeth of iron and claws of bronze, and which devoured and broke in pieces and stamped what was left with its feet"* (Dan. 7:19). Both verses sound like they are describing Rome.

The angel explained to Daniel that this beast would have **ten horns**, perhaps ten different emperors, and later *"there came up **among** them **another horn, a little one**"* (Dan. 7:8a) before whom three would be plucked up by the roots, and *"in this horn were eyes like the eyes of a man, and a mouth speaking great things"* (Dan. 7:8b), which could imply that he will make audacious and arrogant claims. This "little" **eleventh** horn would take over three original ones. Considering a great and evil kingdom that arose from among the ten Roman emperors (without getting bogged down with naming each of the ten, if they were even literal), we might be able to understand that this "Other Little Horn" could represent the **Muslim Turkish Ottoman Empire**, which destroyed the **Christian Byzantine Empire** in 1453.

People nowadays have forgotten how powerful that kingdom was, but it actually destroyed and substituted the Christian empire with a Muslim empire. Both Jews and Christians were expelled, forced to convert to Islam, or killed. In my estimation, this "Other Little Horn" of Daniel 7:8 could also be equivalent to the **First Beast from the Sea** of Revelation 13:2, which is described in similar language: *"And the beast that I saw was like a **leopard**; its feet were like a **bear**'s, and its mouth was like a **lion**'s mouth. And to it the **dragon** gave his power and his throne and great authority."*

Then, after Daniel asked for some clarification, Daniel 7:24 talks about a "Different Horn" that will arise from the former ones: *"… and another shall arise **after them**; he shall be **different from the former ones**, and shall put down three kings"* (Dan. 7:24). Even though this sounds very similar to the description of the above "Other Little Horn," it is not identical. The dominion of the first "Other Little Horn," which I understand represents the historic Muslim Ottoman Empire, would be *"taken away,"* but its life would be *"prolonged for a season and a time"* (v. 12). This new horn can be related to the previous "Other Little Horn," since it also says that he *"had eyes and a mouth that spoke great things…"* but this time it will be worse, since we read that it *"seemed greater than its companions"* (v. 20), thus representing a renewed Muslim Ottoman Empire, until it will be destroyed forever (v. 26).

I also relate this second "Different Horn" to the leader described in Daniel 11:40-45, who clearly seems to describe the future Antichrist. These both could then be related to the **Second Beast from the Earth** in Revelation 13:11-12.

Ultimately, this horn will be forever destroyed *"to the end"* (v. 26), when the heavenly court sits in judgment and takes away his dominion, which could easily place it **in our future**. In addition, this future Beast from the Earth could be seen as a **renewed** Muslim Turkish Ottoman Empire, and could represent the future Antichrist, who will arise from the historic Turkish Ottoman Empire, and who I anticipate will unite the Muslim world under one global caliphate. (See Appendix 1.)

4) The Beasts of Revelation

In a similar manner as I see the birthing of Islam in Daniel 11:31b, 36-39, I believe that the first Beast mentioned in the book of Revelation, the **Beast from the Bottomless Pit,** is also a reference to that historical event. It says that he *"will make war on them* [God's two witnesses] *and conquer them and kill them"* (Rev. 11:7). Islam was given birth by Satan in the early 7th century to supersede the God of the Bible, the true God of both Judaism and Christianity. To see this more clearly, we must look at our history books regarding how this evidently antichristian religion and government system appeared and what it has achieved in the world up to now.

After the first three centuries of Roman persecution against Christians, Emperor Constantine was supposedly converted to Christianity in the 4th century, transforming the multi-deity Roman Empire into a "Christian Empire" and spreading this faith to all its territories towards the east and west, including Israel. Even though we may not agree with many of the things he did and the Christian doctrine that was later established under the name of the Roman "Catholic" (or "universal," from the Greek adjective καθολικός - katholikos) Church, it was God's instrument to spread Christianity to most of the Middle Eastern region and beyond. Constantine moved the Roman capital to Byzantium and renamed it Constantinople, but then it was split off from the Western part of the empire. The eastern part of the empire survived after the fall of the western section, which was overrun during the 5th century (around AD 628) by Germanic and other northern tribes, thus maintaining the name of **Byzantine Empire**. At the same time, much of the farther eastern empire was being conquered by the Persians (Sassanid Empire), so the Byzantine Empire was left only with Asia Minor. That was when **Mohammad** appeared on the scene (622-632), conquering the Arabian Peninsula and spreading Islam by means of war and death.

Soon after Mohammad's death, Jerusalem was taken away from the Byzantine Empire following a siege in 637 led by Abu Ubaidah of the Muslim Rashidun Caliphate. More Muslim conquests were led by other leaders during the 7th and 8th centuries, and in this manner the Muslim religion slowly expanded so as to cover the southern part of the European continent and North Africa, and reached as far east as Iran, Pakistan and Kashimir. Nevertheless, these countries never really became united as one empire until the 15th century under the **Ottoman Empire**. The small extension of the Christian Empire in Asia Minor still stood until Constantinople was totally taken over by the Ottoman Empire in 1453 under the leadership of Mehmed the Conqueror.

At present, even though "Christianity" (including Roman Catholicism, the various Orthodox churches, and Protestantism) is sometimes considered the largest religious affiliation worldwide, true Christianity is probably only minor in size. Most European countries that were previously Christian have now become so secularized that they are being taken over by Islam or atheism. At present, Islam is the fastest growing religion in the world, controlling about 25% of the global population, which represents a large majority in over 50 countries. Islam means "submission" or "surrender," requiring total adherence (even by force) to the precepts of its prophet Mohammad, supposedly revealed to him by Archangel Gabriel (*Jibril*). Its main goal is to eliminate the "infidels" (emphasizing Jews and Christians) and to impose this religious/political faith upon the whole world through *Jihad*, or holy war. It also teaches a substitute end-time theology of a **Mahdi**, their prophesied "redeemer" or messiah, which clearly represents **an Antichrist figure**. They believe that Islam will finally triumph, and that this person will establish the ultimate "*ummah*" or Caliphate, something very similar to the Messianic Kingdom.

We can read in Revelation 11:7 that the Beast from the Bottomless Pit, namely **Islam**, will be the one to conquer the "**two witnesses**," who I believe represent both **Israel** and the **Church**, as discussed previously. This could easily mean that the religious and political Islamic ideology that has proceeded from the bottomless pit would succeed, at some point, in dominating Christianity and Judaism. Historically, the first "3½ days" of their testimony could represent the time Christianity controlled large parts of the world through the Christian Roman and Byzantine Empires, while Israel was still serving as a witness of God's Law during its dispersion. The two "witnesses" were then both spiritually "killed" by Islam, or the "Beast from the Bottomless Pit." Islam managed to maintain control of the Holy Land, in spite of the Crusades,[70] while their symbolic dead

---

[70] Even though Christian crusaders tried retaking Jerusalem from the Muslims, they only succeeded for about 100 years.

bodies (Christianity and Judaism) laid in Jerusalem for a symbolic 3½ days. Muslim armies symbolically refused to let them be "buried" (or honored), but rejoiced over their destruction because these two people groups *"had been a torment to those who dwell on earth"* (Rev. 11:10). We often hear how Muslims still *"make merry and exchange presents"* when a terrorist attack against Jews and Christians is successful.

It is important to note that Muslims believe that any territory they previously held and later lost to Christianity or Judaism must be reconquered for Islam again, including the European countries that they had once held. Even if some people allege that Islam is a religion of "peace," Islam's highest and most profound goal is to kill and destroy Christianity and Judaism. It is permitted to use deceit, violence, or any other means necessary. Muslim societies are intentional in teaching their children to hate Jews and Christians, and teach them that it is their duty to kill them "for Allah's honor." According to Islam, these faiths had been effectively conquered and superseded, and must remain so.

In Revelation we read about the same two closely-related beasts identified in Daniel 7, which here are also named the Beast from the Sea: *"And I saw a beast rising out of the sea, with ten horns and seven heads, with ten diadems on its horns and blasphemous names on its heads"* (Rev. 13:1), and the Beast from the Earth: *"Then I saw another beast rising out of the earth. It had two horns like a lamb and it spoke like a dragon"* (Rev. 13:11). As also mentioned previously, my personal interpretation is that the First Beast from the Sea can be related to the **historic Muslim Turkish Ottoman Empire**, which has already come and gone, but the Second Beast from the Earth will present itself as a **revived Muslim Turkish Ottoman Empire** under the rule of the *Mahdi* or Antichrist.

Regarding the **First Beast from the Sea**, we must remember that the Christian Byzantine Empire arose directly from the Roman Empire initiated by Constantine the Great, which lasted from the 4th to 15th centuries (with various extensions of territory and domination). When the Muslim Ottoman Empire conquered it in the 15th century, the dominion of this new empire eventually covered an even greater territory than the Christian one (western Asia, much of southeast Europe and the Caucasus, parts of central and southwestern Europe, North Africa and the Horn of Africa, including Israel), which lasted about 600 years until the early 20th century. During the 16th and 17th centuries, at the height of its power under the reign of Suleiman the Magnificent, the Ottoman Empire was a multinational, multilingual empire. Suleiman instituted what many call the "Golden Age" of the Ottoman Empire in terms of law, education, and the arts. He ruled with a strong arm over 15 to 25 million people during the 16th century, and his capital city was the previously Christian Byzantine capital city of Constantinople (which was renamed as Istanbul in 1930, when the modern country of Turkey changed its capital to Ankara). Nevertheless, he had great reverence for Jerusalem, which was at the time a Muslim center, and he rebuilt the city's outer fallen walls between 1537 and 1541. But this empire was broken up at the end of World War I, and many of its lands were distributed to form some the modern Middle Eastern nations as we know them today, including Jordan, Lebanon, Syria, Iraq, Kuwait, and modern Turkey.

Revelation 13:11-18 then describes what I have termed as the **Second Beast from the Earth**. This one is similar to the First Beast and will have two 2 horns like a lamb but speak like a dragon. In other words, it will look as defenseless as a lamb but be a spokesman for Satan and its Islamic ideology. The First Beast will temporarily suffer a mortal wound, which can be represented by the "death" of the Ottoman Empire when it fell at the end of World War I and simply became the modern nation of Turkey. But the life of this beast will survive, and be prolonged until, or raised again in, the last days, as Daniel 7:12 says: *"As for the rest of the **beasts**, their dominion was taken away, but **their lives were prolonged** for a season and a time."*

Thus, this Second Beast can "come back to life" as a renewed version of the fallen Muslim Turkish Ottoman Empire, perhaps including Iran, the political Vatican, the European Union, and the global inter-governmental organization of the United Nations. We should note that the global governing body of the United Nations, which was formed in 1948 at the end of World War II, does not follow Christian values, but is controlled almost entirely by the Muslim nations worldwide. The Second Beast will exercise all the authority of the First Beast and will make the people of the earth worship the Beast from the Bottomless Pit (Islam). Some outstanding leader may appear and perform miraculous signs, deceiving the world and telling them to worship the image of the First Beast who can speak, which could be merely a reference to the teachings of Islam in the Coran and other writings, according to the Muslim Sharia law. Those who do not worship Allah will be punished and slain.

We must be aware that Turkey's present leader, Recep Tayyip Erdogan, seeks to become another Caliph and transform it into a new global Turkish Ottoman Empire. He also wants to re-establish Turkey's grip and control over Jerusalem and the Temple Mount, and sees himself as the "father of an Ottoman caliphate that will one day return to Jerusalem," as stated by Nadav Shragai in an *Israel Hayom* website article.[71] During the summer of 2019, Turkey was actively involved in running Arab youth camps in order to

---

[71] Naday Shragai, *Turkey's Target: The Temple Mount*, Israel Hayom, https://www.israelhayom.com /opinions/turkeys-target-the-temple-mount/ (Accessed July 10, 2019).

deepen Turkish influence over Jerusalem. According to another article on the *Israel Hayom* website, the Muslim group *Our Heritage* "operates in east Jerusalem as an arm of the Turkish government. Its goals are to promote the Turkish agenda among the population of east Jerusalem and deepen the historical and cultural legacy of the Ottoman Empire in Jerusalem, which they call 'preserving Ottoman history in Jerusalem for future generations.'"[72]

Nevertheless, Iran seems to have more influence than Turkey at the moment, but Iran may consider joining Turkey in this endeavor, since both have the same agenda, though each want to hold the reins of power. Maybe some leader will unite Shiism and Sunnism, creating an alleged "world peace." This seems to be the main purpose of an event held in Ankara, Turkey in September 2019 titled "Congress on the Future of Islamic World and Palestine."[73] During the conference, the chairman of a Turkish-Shiite association, Kadir Arakas, said that "Israel must be dissolved and destroyed," and that "resistance in Palestine is important" during the "weakest period of Israel's history." The AhlulBayt News Agency (ABNA) reported that the conference was organized by the **Saadat Islamic Unity Research Center** in Turkey, bringing together more than 70 foreign guests from 20 countries. According to ABNA, the conference held the following panels: "Al-Quds [Jerusalem] is the Most Important and Fundamental Issue of the Islamic World; Islamic Unity: The Muslims' Only Way for the Future; The Impact of the Palestinian

[72] Yori Yalon, *Turkish Organization teaches Arab kids from East Jerusalem that Israel is theirs,* Israel Hayom, https://www.israelhayom.com/2019/07/09/turkish-organization-teaches-arab-kids-from-east-jerusalem-that-israel-is-theirs/ (Accessed July 10, 2019).

[73] Benjamin Weinthal, *Call to Destroy Israel at Islamist Conference in Ankara,* The Jerusalem Post, https://www.jpost.com/Arab-Israeli-Conflict/Call-to-destroy-Israel-at-Islamist-conference-in-Ankara-602442, (Accessed September 23, 2019).

Issue on the Islamic World and the Responsibilities of the Islamic Ummah [worldwide Caliphate]; World Status and Issues of Islam, Problems and Solutions; and Concerning the Greater Middle East Plan / Deal of the Century Agreement, its Goals and Supporters; and Conditions for Implementation of the **Islamic Unity Plan**."

On the other hand, the United Nations has already submitted itself to Islam, providing it with a legal venue for obtaining world domination. When Israel was reborn in 1948, this governing body barely granted its approval. It was only by God's grace, and a few Christian nations who still had some political clout, that Israel was able to become a new nation. Nevertheless, the United Nations and the political Vatican have always been trying to internationalize Jerusalem and prevent it from returning to Israel's hands. After 70 years, only two nations, United States and Guatemala, dared to officially recognize Jerusalem as Israel's capital, in opposition to the will of the UN, Vatican, and the Muslim nations. The Beast from the Bottomless Pit (Islam) is still trying to destroy the nation of Israel and claim Jerusalem for itself. The European Union is also usually identified on the side of Muslim nations rather than with the United States and Israel, and more so now since its borders have become so open and overrun by Muslim immigrants. These are presently establishing themselves in huge numbers and taking over the European governments by means of threats, blackmails, and violence. It is now almost impossible to speak against Islam or take any legal action against it because it is classified as Islamophobia and termed as "illegal" and punishable by law.

An article in *Gatestone Institute*[74] reports that the UN has already

---

[74] Judith Bergman, *UN Launches All-out War on Free Speech*, Gatestone Institute, https://www. gatestone institute.org/ 14516/united-nations-free-speech (Accessed July 10, 2019).

approved a number of measures to supposedly prevent Islamophobia, but this is really a cover for protecting Islam from any kind of criticism. "Pakistan has already presented a six-point plan to address the new manifestations of racism and faith-based hatred, especially Islamophobia, at the United Nations headquarters. The presentation was organized by Pakistan along with Turkey, the Holy See and the UN." Moreover, Pakistan alleges that because of Islamophobia, it has itself created the concept of anti-Semitism and other forms of apartheid. So, together with the UN and the Vatican, they are creating an action plan "to reverse the tide of hate and bigotry that threatens to undermine social solidarity and peaceful co-existence." These measures sound commendable, if they were not a disguise to keep any and all criticism of Islam off the media and social platforms, and probably even out of private places of gathering and individual minds.

I personally interpret that the Second Beast won't officially appear on the scene until after the saints have been resurrected (or "raptured"), which is to be discussed in the next section. In any case, he will look like a lamb but speak like a dragon, and will force the world to submit to the First Beast of the Sea, namely the original Muslim Empire (Rev. 13:11-18). *"Also it causes all, both small and great, both rich and poor, both free and slave, to be marked on the right hand or the forehead"* (Rev. 13:16).

At this present moment in time, the two most powerful nations that oppose the formation of this evil dominion are United States and Israel, representing the Christian and Jewish worlds, termed by Iran as the Big Satan (the U.S.) and Little Satan (Israel). It is evident that this new global Muslim Empire or Caliphate cannot happen until United States and Israel either submit or disappear. But once the true Christians and Jews are out of the way after the resurrection, the new

Muslim Ottoman Empire can easily force everyone to submit to its dominion and be sealed with its "number." God warns that those who receive this seal will also drink the wine of His wrath when the "Bowls of Wrath" are poured out upon the earth. In the meantime, God calls all His saints to endure and to keep His commandments and their faith in Jesus, those who have the **"seal" of the Holy Spirit**. Ultimately, the Antichrist's time will come to a completion when Jesus returns to establish His Kingdom (Dan. 7:22).

5) **Man of Lawlessness still restrained**

If my suppositions are correct, most (but not all) of Daniel's beasts have already appeared on the world stage and have fallen away. Two of the mentioned Beasts of Revelation have also made their entrance onstage, namely the Beast from the Bottomless Pit (in the form of Islam), and the First Beast from the Sea (as the ancient Muslim Turkish Ottoman Empire, which disappeared after World War I). I understand that the **Second Beast from the Earth** (the soon-to-be-revived Sunni-Shiite Muslim Caliphate, plus the United Nations, European Union, and the Vatican) is already in its formation process and can easily become fully empowered. We have not yet been able to identify a single world leader who might fill the role of the Antichrist, but we can see that the above powerful entities have already created his platform from where he can easily effectuate his mandate. There is also the probability that this "persona non-grata" could be just a government under a coalition of leaders, rather than a single leader.

When will this Antichrist take over the governments of the world? The Apostle Paul discusses this issue about the timing of when the "Man of Lawlessness" will appear. He introduces the topic by saying:

*"Now concerning the coming of our Lord Jesus Christ [the Parousia] and our being gathered together to him [the resurrection], we ask you, brothers, not to be quickly shaken in mind or alarmed, either by a spirit or a spoken word, or a letter seeming to be from us, to the effect **that the day of the Lord has come**"* (2 Thess. 2:1-2).

Before getting into the topic of the Antichrist, we should mention that there is a discussion regarding the purpose of this letter. Walvoord alleges that Paul needed to clarify various issues because he was countering the incipient "false doctrine" of Postribulationism, and that he had already taught that believers would be raptured before the final persecution of the saints.[75] There is no foundation for this allegation, so this is pure conjecture. F. F. Bruce[76] believes that what was bewildering the believers was that some were teaching that Christ had already come. That is why Paul had to set them straight. Nevertheless, the Greek word in verse 2 helps us understand what Paul's real concern was. We read that the notion Paul needed to correct was that the "day of Christ" (*emera tou Xristou*) was **"at hand"** (*enésteken*). This term should not be translated as "already come" in past tense, because it really speaks about an imminent action in the very near future. It seems like some people were saying that Jesus' return was going to be very soon, so Paul had to give them a clear picture of the events that needed to occur **before** Jesus returned to establish His Kingdom.

Another aspect that has created controversy in verse 1 is the fact

---

[75] Walvoord, *The Rapture Question* (Grand Rapids, MI: Zondervan Publ. House, 1979), 238.

[76] F. F. Bruce, "1 & 2 Thessalonians" in *Word Biblical Commentary* vol. 45 (Mexico City: Thomas Nelson, Inc., 1982), 166.

that we see the *"coming of our Lord Jesus Christ"* mentioned together with *"our being gathered together to him."* Evidently, Paul referred to Christ's *Parousia,* which literally means His advent or presence, right before he referred to our *"episounagoge,"* or our being assembled or gathered to Him. Since Paul is mentioning both things in the same sentence and in this order, we can get a very confused picture regarding these two separate events. I don't believe that this can imply a simultaneous action (as some Postribulationists believe), just as it cannot reflect a chronological order of events (which would be illogically inverted), but that these two phrases simply refer to the entire end-time scenario in a general manner, including the resurrection of the saints **prior** to Christ's second coming (*Parousia*) to establish His Kingdom. Paul had clearly told the believers in Colossi that *"when Christ who is your life appears* ["phanero"], *then you also will appear with him in glory"* (Col. 3:4), implying that His saints will be accompanying Christ to earth at His Parousia **after** being raised from the dead during a previous event, not during the same event.

2 Thessalonians 2:3-12 has also caused great controversy, since the unclear wording could be interpreted in different ways regarding the coming of the Antichrist. Is the resurrection of the saints **before** or **after** the Man of Lawlessness is revealed? Will God's people actually be around at the time of the Antichrist's government, or will they already be gone by that time? It is interesting to note that Paul used *"parousia"* for Jesus' "coming" (2 Thess. 2:1) and as well as for the Antichrist's "coming" (2 Thess. 2:9). He also used *"apokalupto"* for when Christ will be "revealed" from heaven with His angels (2 Thess. 1:7) and also when the Antichrist is to be "revealed" (in 2 Thess. 2:3, 6, and 8).

Verse 3 says, according to the ESV: **"that day will not come"** unless the Man of Lawlessness has been first revealed (*apokalupthe*).

But the Greek text never uses the phrase "that day will not come," only an implied reference to **"the day of Christ"** (*emera tou Xristou*) previously mentioned in verse 2, or the day when Christ returns in glory, clearly **not the day of resurrection**.

> *"...to the effect that the **day of the Lord** has come. For **[the Parousia]** will not come, unless the rebellion comes first, and the man of lawlessness is revealed, the son of destruction... "* (2 Thess. 2:2-3).

This means that the Man of Lawlessness will be revealed before Jesus' return in glory (the Parousia), but not that he will be revealed before the resurrection. This is very important! This complements verses 6-8, which clarify that the Antichrist **can't** be revealed **until something is out of the way**. After that, he will reveal himself. Now let's look at these verses, according to the ESV:

> *"And you know what is **restraining him** now so that he may be revealed in his time. For the mystery of lawlessness is already at work. Only he **who now restrains it** will do so until he is **out of the way**. And **then the lawless one will be revealed**"* (2 Thess. 2:6-8).

Regarding the identity of this enigmatic "restrainer," Paul states that he had discussed this with the believers when he was still with them (v. 6), but because we do not have those specific words, we must analyze the ones that are registered here. F. F. Bruce details a few theories.[77] He refers to Tertullian's argument (in *De Resurrection* from the 2nd to 3rd century) that the restrainer was the Roman state, and that when it is removed it will be divided into ten different kingdoms,

---

[77] Bruce, 171.

which will then bring on the Antichrist. In this manner, the Roman government provided structure and stability while in power, but afterwards, things would turn chaotic. Chrysostom agreed with this (in *Homily on 2 Thessalonians*), "because if Paul had meant the Spirit, he would have said so plainly and not obscurely...but because he meant the Roman Empire, he naturally glanced at it, speaking covertly and darkly..."

Bruce states that he shares Tertullian's opinion based on the supposition that Paul considered that the imperial Roman power at the time was what provided order and social control so that the Gospel could continue to spread. He says that we can see this idea when Paul insisted in Romans 13:1-7 that God had established governmental authorities to protect law-abiding citizens, and that they must be subject to these God-ordained rulers. Based on this view, Bruce concludes: "When the restraint of law and order was relaxed, the forces of lawlessness would have it all their own way, under the direction of the 'man of lawlessness.'"[78] But Romans 13 does not mean that Paul was thinking in those terms, nor does it explain why the Antichrist was not revealed after the Roman Empire fell. There have been many occasions and centuries of political chaos in this world, yet the Man of Lawlessness has still not taken power.

But Darby reinterpreted Chrysostom's perspective when he said (in *Notes on the Epistles to the Thessalonians*):[79] "...the thing which restrained then is not that which restrains now...At present, the hindrance is still the existence of the governments established by God in the world; and God will maintain them as long as there is here below the gathering of His church. Viewed in this light, the

---

[78] Ibid, 177.

[79] Ibid.

hindrance is, at the bottom, the presence of the church and of the Holy Spirit on the earth."

I must admit that I agree with Darby here, because this text makes more sense if we interpret the identity of the "restrainer" as the Holy Spirit through Christ's Church. Even though the "rebellion" (*apostasía*) will be evident to Christians before the resurrection, the Man of Lawlessness can't reveal himself as the world dictator until after the Holy Spirit is removed from the earth. **Then** the man of lawlessness, or son of destruction, can establish his reign until Jesus returns in glory with His saints. And when He comes, the Antichrist will be destroyed *"with the breath of his mouth and bring to nothing by the appearance of his coming* [Parousia]*"* (2 Thess. 2:8).

Thus, I believe that the Antichrist is presently being restrained by the Holy Spirit's presence through Israel and the Church, and will remain so until the moment when Jesus gathers up His people. The Antichrist cannot establish his reign of terror until after the saints are *"out of the way."* He will then have free reign, until he is finally destroyed on "the day of Christ" (*emera tou Xristou*). But before the resurrection, Christians will be experiencing the **"tribulation of those days"** due to a general rebellion or "falling away" (*apostasía*). The resurrection will be at the end of this latter-day tribulation, while the short period that follows the resurrection ("one hour," according to Revelation 17:12) cannot be classified as "tribulation." During that post-resurrection time, everyone will be willingly devoted to worshiping and serving the Antichrist: *"… they refused to love the truth and so be saved. Therefore God sends them a strong delusion, so that they may believe what is false…"* (2 Thess. 2:10-11). They will all be willing to have the "mark of the Beast."

We may be facing difficult times ahead while the *apostasía* and the Antichrist gain strength. We may also be able to identify how the different players on the board are getting into place. Now is the time when Christians must define themselves as to which side they are on, **whether for God and His Messiah, or for the Antichrist.** Many Christians may depart from their faith, as they are influenced by deceitful spirits that will abound more and more.

> *"Now the Spirit expressly says that **in later times** some will depart from the faith by devoting themselves to deceitful spirits and teachings of demons, through the insincerity of liars whose consciences are seared..."* (1 Tim. 4:1-2).

Will we try and appease the growing Muslim powers, joining the new and blasphemous "Chrislam" movement, or do we stay steadfast and true in the midst of our persecutions and tribulations? *"Therefore we ourselves boast about you in the churches of God for your **steadfastness and faith** in all your persecutions and in the afflictions that you are enduring"* (2 Thess. 1:4).

After the resurrection of the saints, this "son of destruction" will finally sit in the *"temple of God"* and proclaim himself to be God (2 Thess. 2:4). This is often used to defend the idea that the Antichrist will be Jewish, and that the Temple must be rebuilt before the Antichrist is to be revealed. But as stated before, the term *"naon tou Theo"* can refer to **any type of sanctuary dedicated to a divinity**, and the ***Al Aksa Mosque*** fits this description perfectly. Here is where the Antichrist will proclaim himself to be God. Once Israel and the Church have been removed, the Antichrist will have all the liberty to sit in the "temple of God" (the mosque on the Temple Mount) and proclaim himself to be "God" without any opposition. He will be empowered by Satan, since *"the coming of the lawless one is by the activity of Satan with all power and false signs and wonders, and with all wicked deception for those who are perishing..."* (2 Thess. 2:9-10).

We can compare this with the book of Revelation, chapters 13 to 18. These are not a chronological continuation of the previous chapters, but a clarification of the previous ones for our benefit. It says that when the First Beast from the Sea is to be in power (the Muslim Turkish Ottoman Empire), humanity is asked two important questions: *"Who is like the beast, and who can fight against it?"* (Rev. 13:4). These are evidently rhetorical questions, since the expected answer from those who had given themselves over to worship the First Beast after receiving his authority from the dragon (Satan) would be: "no one." But those Turks only had their authority because God gave it to them, as it says: *"**it was allowed** to make war on the saints and to conquer them. And **authority was given it** over every tribe and people and language and nation"* (Rev. 13:7). Even though it says **every** tribe and nation, we can interpret that this means the **Biblical nations around the Middle and Near East**. The next verse says that *"all who dwell on earth will worship it."* This could also be just a hyperbolic rendering of reality. The text clarifies that **not everyone** worshipped the beast, because this only includes *"everyone **whose name has not been written** before the foundation of the world in the book of life of the Lamb who was slain"* (Rev. 13:8). Those whose names **are** written in the Lamb's Book of Life did **not** worship this beast. God's people were taken captive or slain for their faith, such as the almost two million Armenian Christians who were murdered when the Ottoman Empire began to crumble at the end of World War I. *"Here is a call for the **endurance and faith** of the saints"* (Rev. 13:10). (See Appendix 2.)

E. Signs of the End Times

1) The Seals and Trumpets of Revelation

As stated previously, my understanding is that the symbolic **First to Fifth Seals** in Revelation 6:1-11 describe the "normal tribulations" that began in the past and are still ongoing, which include: 1) wars and conquests, 2) tyrants and assassinations, 3) financial disasters and famines, 4) death and pestilences, and 5) martyrdom of God's people. These also correspond to what Jesus described in the Olivet Discourse: *"For nation will rise against nation, and kingdom against kingdom, and there will be famines and earthquakes in various places…"* (Matt. 24:7). Luke adds "pestilences" to the list (Lk. 21:11), while both also include "martyrdom" (Matt. 24: 9; Lk. 21:16). This is precisely what has been happening ever since Jesus spoke those words. And then He clarified: *"See that you are not alarmed, for this must take place, but the end is not yet"* (Matt. 24:6).

During the long interim before the end (Lk. 21:12-24), the disciples would be persecuted, Jerusalem would be destroyed and trampled on by the Gentiles, and the Jewish people would be dispersed **until the times of the Gentiles reach their fulfillment**. I understand that **all** these things represent the *"great distress upon the earth,"* especially for the Jewish people, as an extended period of time, not seven literal years. And while Christians wait for the final events to unfold, we must reach the rest of the world with the Gospel. The Internet has made the Word accessible to most anyone who may want to read it. What is still perhaps necessary is to translate it to the remaining languages for people groups who still don't have it and can't yet read it.

In Luke, we read that Jesus also included *"terrors and great signs from heaven"* in that list of events (Lk. 21:11), which sounds very similar to the Sixth Seal. Revelation 6:12 describes the **Sixth Seal** in this way:

> *"When he opened the sixth seal, I looked, and behold, there was a great earthquake, and the sun became black as sackcloth, the full moon became like blood, and the stars of the sky fell to the earth as the fig tree sheds its winter fruit when shaken by a gale. The sky vanished like a scroll that is being rolled up, and every mountain and island was removed from its place"* (Rev. 6:12-14).

Even though the *"kings of the earth"* and all peoples may feel that this is *"the great day of their wrath"* (referring to the wrath of Him *"who is seated on the throne, and from the wrath of the Lamb"*), it really isn't, because that will come later, once God's people are out of the way. But what does all this refer to? If taken literally, it would represent the **total annihilation of all creation**, because it says that all the celestial bodies are cast out of their place and the land masses on earth disappear. No one could survive such a catastrophe! The picture is horrifying! But is this really to be taken literally? What if this Sixth Seal is also to be understood metaphorically? What if it is just enough suffering to make unbelievers tremble and repent? After all, the rest of Revelation still describes human life as it continues on earth, and we don't see an absolute disappearance of all things, which will not occur until much later with the new heavens and new earth.

I propose that the Sixth Seal is just a **prelude** to the **Seventh Seal**, which includes the **signs** of the **Seven Trumpets** as its sub-components. These could represent global crises that will happen simultaneously throughout the world, and large numbers of people will die, but it will not be a total annihilation as such. I don't know how much time will transpire during this whole process, but I don't see much distinction between them in regards to timing. Even though we presently don't see the cataclysmic changes in the sun, moon, and stars as described above, the Trumpets will announce events sufficiently impacting so that Revelation 8:1 begins with a profound silence in heaven for *"half an hour."* This pause seems to describe a sense of foreboding and awe among the angelic beings regarding the disasters that are about to ensue on earth. An angel put incense into a golden censor together with the prayers of the saints, and then added fire from the altar to it, *"and threw it on the earth, and there were peals of thunder, rumblings, flashes of lightning, and an earthquake"* (Rev. 8:5). This holy "bomb" will be in vindication for all the suffering of God's people, and He will also be answering all the saint's prayers that have come up to Him through the ages, which will be used in retribution for all those who opposed His people. (See Appendix 3.)

Do the described actions and results of the Trumpets just represent something in a symbolic way, just as the First to Fifth Seals are evidently symbolic? Let us consider what Revelation says about these Seven Trumpets and some possibilities of their significance. The first **Three Trumpets** describe calamities in which a third of all land, oceans, and rivers are destroyed. Could this represent the widespread contamination of earth, seas, and rivers that has already been evident for the past several decades? The pollution has ruined much of our agricultural land, many of the important ocean coral reefs, and a great many rivers that are source for our drinking water. The **Fourth Trumpet** describes a darkening of the sun, moon, and stars, which may not have anything to do with a literal event, but with cloudiness caused by heavy air pollution. There has also been much preoccupation about increasing danger from destructive solar rays due to the disappearance of our ozone layer, more frequent and greater solar flares, besides possible global warming as a result of increased carbon gas emissions.

The **Fifth Trumpet** describes evil powers from the bottomless pit that are going to be torturing those *"who do not have the seal of God on their foreheads"* for "5 months" (Rev. 9:4). It also speaks about certain creatures preparing for battle, which seem to resemble modern tanks and warplanes, and whose leader is clearly Satan (Abaddon and Apollyon). Could this refer to the dictatorships and modern warfare during the Second World War? This was the deadliest military conflict in history, and only the allied Christian nations were able to stop this evil advance. An estimated total of 70 to 85 million people perished, which was about 3% of the world population (estimated to be near 2.3 billion at 1940).

The **Sixth Trumpet** also describes a war, but this time in the region surrounding the Euphrates River. Might this refer to the later wars in Iraq and the Middle East that have been ongoing for several decades since World War II, mainly due to Islamist efforts to dominate the world? It certainly seems like demonic spirits were released at the time of the destruction of the Twin Towers in New York and the subsequent Iraqi war. On the other hand, could the reference to fire, smoke, and sulfur refer to weapons of mass destruction which have already been used extensively in the area? (Rev. 9:18). Could this imply that there will be a future nuclear war? If all this is true, have we already seen some of the effects of the Sixth Seal and the first Six Trumpets? (See Appendix 4).

To better understand the significance of these signs, we must see what the sound of trumpets signified in ancient Biblical times. They were sounded on many different occasions, but the most common practice among the nations was to sound the trumpets as a **warning of danger** (Jer. 6:1, 17; Ezek. 33:3-6) and to gather their **armies for**

battle (Josh. 6:4-5; Judg. 7:18; Neh. 4:20). But in Israel, trumpets or *shofarim* (ram's horns) were more often used for **assembling God's people** before Him (Ex. 19:18-19), for calling them to **repent** and be **consecrated in prayer and fasting** (Lev. 25:9; Joel 2:15-16), and for **celebrating** and **singing praises to His name** (Psa. 81:3; Psa. 150:3). In the future, trumpets will also be used to **declare that God will save His people** (Num. 10:9; Zech. 9:12-17), and then also to announce the arrival of **God's wrath against the nations** (Zeph. 1:15-18). Just as trumpets were used to announce **new kings** in Israel (2 Sam. 15:10; 1 Kgs. 1:39), they will also be used to declare that the **Lord sits above on His holy throne** (Psa. 47:5-9).

All of the above common practices seem to be happening **simultaneously** during the seven eschatological Trumpets: The text seems to describe a huge amassing of armies for war, including weapons of mass destruction and nuclear bombs with horrendous results. God will be announcing to His people that He will save them and gather them to Himself, but also warning unbelievers that if they don't repent, they will see His wrath. And He will be announcing that He is Lord of all the earth and is seated on His throne! The first six trumpet calls are clear admonitions for the nations to repent before the Father calls His people up to Him. After the **Seventh Trumpet**, it will be too late for unbelievers to repent. God will have given them sufficient warning so that none will have an excuse. From then on, He will sit on His holy throne for their coming judgment.

On the other hand, are the trumpet sounds really going to be audible? God produced an audible trumpet sound in Genesis for all to hear and fear: *"On the morning of the third day there were thunders and lightnings and a thick cloud on the mountain and a **very loud trumpet blast**, so that all the people in the camp trembled"* (Ex. 19:16). He is still able to produce a trumpet blast so loud that all the people of the earth will hear it and tremble in recognition of God's power and presence, and also as a warning of impending doom for the unrepentant.

A powerful YouTube recording was made in 2016 when many people in Jerusalem heard a long series of trumpet sounds blaring from a circular ring of clouds in the sky.[80] Some even witness of similar sounds in many different parts of the globe! This was a literal sound, heard and recorded by many people on their phones, stirring wonderment and fear in their hearts. Are these just explainable atmospheric effects, or are they the first of the signs that will appear in heaven? Does this mean that the Trumpets have actually started sounding? I must admit that this is very compelling!

As mentioned previously, we are already suffering from the effects of global warming, destructive super-storms and hurricanes, uncontainable forest fires, huge tsunamis, widespread water, land, and air contaminations, reduction in the ozone layer, frequent and stronger earthquakes, and many other upheavals in nature, killing many thousands upon thousands of people worldwide. Scientists predict only an increase in all these things. We have also seen more red "blood" moons than usual, though those are a normal result of celestial rotations. Still, we are not yet experiencing destruction to the degree that a third of the land, water, and humankind has been destroyed. On the other hand, was World War II part of these events, which definitely resulted in the death of millions of people worldwide, including the Middle East wars that have also killed many thousands of people? Al-Qaida and ISIS (Islamic State) terrorists certainly fit the picture, even though they have been slightly contained. And everyone is justifiably fearful about what a wide nuclear war could do, which is why the US and Israel (and other nations) are trying

---

[80] YouTube, https://youtube.com/watch?v=5ErbClbS460 (accessed January 31, 2019).

to keep Iran from obtaining nuclear weapons. Turkey is already showing its suppressed aggression and blindsiding the Western world with a renewed Islamist hegemonic thrust. But at this moment, the righteous are still suffering along with the unrighteous, and the Jews have not yet believed in their Messiah. Things are probably going to progress little by little, and these might just be the beginning. Perhaps we will soon experience stronger natural disasters, some type of nuclear destruction, and more calamitous signs in heaven.

Regarding an **increase of evil** in this world, Paul told Timothy that in the last days, *"there will come times of difficulty"* (2 Tim. 3:1). He described humanity in general terms:

> *"For people will be lovers of self, lovers of money, proud, arrogant, abusive, disobedient to their parents, ungrateful, unholy, heartless, unappeasable, slanderous, without self-control, brutal, not loving good, treacherous, reckless, swollen with conceit, lovers of pleasure rather than lovers of God, having the appearance of godliness, but denying its power…"* (2 Tim. 3:2-5).

Even though these things have always existed, it is hard to deny that we are seeing a greater proliferation of these characteristics even in our own Western culture than ever before, without even considering demonic evil groups and rogue nations. In any case, these signs should make us **hopeful**, not distressed. Jesus said that when we see these things, we can be comforted by knowing that **our redemption is near**. Is it this generation that will not pass until all is fulfilled?

2) Salvation/Redemption of Israel

Let us now look at what is described between the Sixth and Seventh Seals, starting in Revelation 7. This chapter continues the narration begun in the previous chapter, describing a special angel that comes from the east who tells the angels to **hold back the destruction** and to **wait.** We must be aware that a new chapter does not necessarily mean that there is a break in thought or timing, since the chapter numbers are merely artificial divisions. Revelation 7:1 begins with the Greek words *"kai metá tavta"* (translated above in the ESV as "after this"). This Greek phrase actually connects one thing with the next, which in this case unites the events of the Sixth Seal with the "sealing" of the Jewish people. *"Metá"* more often carries the idea of a closeness or link between two things, rather than a separation. This phrase could be better understood to mean "**and together with these things**," or "**and in accompaniment with these things**." Clearly, there is a direct correlation between the Sixth and Seventh Seals. They should be described as occurring **during or alongside** the previous one, rather than after. Thus, my understanding is that what follows in Revelation 7 will occur **while** the Sixth and Seventh Seals are being opened and the heavenly signs begin to occur.

> "**[kai metá tavta – Together with these things]**
> *I saw four angels standing at the four corners of the earth…*
> *Then I saw another angel ascending from the rising of the sun,*
> *with the seal of the living God, and he called with a loud voice*
> *to the four angels who had been given power to harm earth and*
> *sea, saying,* '**Do not harm the earth** *or the sea or the*
> *trees,* **until we have sealed the servants of our**
> **God** *on their foreheads'"* (Rev. 7:1-3).

I believe that God will obtain Israel's attention during the upheavals of the Sixth and Seventh Seals in order to reveal Himself to His people and then "seal" them with His Holy Spirit. The Jewish people have always looked for special divine signs, and Jesus even referred to this. He once mentioned the sign of Jonah as something that illustrated His death and resurrection (Matt. 12:39-40). Thus, these signs of the Sixth and Seventh Seals will be such eye-openers for the Jewish people that they will recognize them as the announcement of their long-awaited Messiah. They will see these as the "footsteps of the Messiah" (Psalm 89:51), which is a common Jewish concept, and they will finally believe that Jesus is their Messiah.

In this manner, the Sixth Seal does **not** represent the "Day of Wrath," as many theologians propose, but the time when Israel will begin to consider that the Messiah is about to come! Revelation 7 describes 144,000 symbolic people among Israel who will then receive God's seal of the Holy Spirit, evidently representing the **whole community of Israel** that will come to the saving knowledge of Jesus as their promised Messiah. This does not contradict the need that everyone needs to make their own decision, but that Israel as a community will believe **in a unified manner**.

What I also see as very significant is that verse 14 identifies these people as *"the ones coming out of the **great tribulation**."* This is the only place in the entire book of Revelation where the term is used, precisely regarding the Jewish people. At this point, they are identified as washed in the blood of the Lamb: *"...They have washed their robes and made them white in the blood of the Lamb"* (Rev. 7:14).

This moment of their salvation is also described by the prophet Zechariah, the moment when the nation of Israel **will look upon Him whom they have pierced** and mourn as one mourns *"for* *an only child"* (Zech. 12:10). The following verses even describe **how** this will happen!

> *"And I will pour out on the house of David and the inhabitants of Jerusalem a **spirit of grace and pleas for mercy**, so that, when they look on me, on him whom they have pierced, they shall mourn for him, as one **mourns for an only child**, and weep bitterly over him, as one **weeps over a firstborn"** (Zech. 12:10).*

> *"On that day the **mourning in Jerusalem** will be as great as the mourning for Hadad-rimmon in the plain of Megiddo. The land shall mourn, **each family by itself**: the family of the house of David by itself, **and their wives by themselves**; the family of the house of Nathan by itself, and their wives by themselves…"* (Zech. 12:11-12).

Even though there has been a gradual increase in Jews coming to the realization that Jesus is their prophesied Messiah, at some moment in the future, entire **families** will **individually** mourn and weep in recognition of their sin of rejecting Jesus, as they receive this glorious revelation. It will not come by anything externally, whether by the teaching of their rabbi or by the preaching of the Gospel. Each family will receive a direct revelation from God. **This will be the most epic moment in all of Jewish history!** How God will do this is impossible to know, but their centuries of denial and rebellion will suddenly come to an end, and they will realize their horrible mistake. At that moment, *"there shall be a fountain opened for the house of David and the inhabitants of Jerusalem, to cleanse them from sin and uncleanness"* (Zech. 13:1). I also believe that the reference to "prophets" who will be ashamed of their prophecies refers to teachers and rabbis who for centuries have taught against Jesus, and they will have to admit, *"I am no prophet"* (Zech. 13:5).

On the other hand, I also interpret that the previous verses in Zechariah 12:1-9 have already been fulfilled, and these do not represent something that will need to occur in a future time. I understand that they describe the way in which Israel was to return and reclaim the land. It says that **Judah will be saved first** (12:7), referring to the physical restoration of Judah in the land, and then **afterwards Jerusalem will be rescued** (12:8), so *"that the glory of the house of David and the glory of the inhabitants of Jerusalem may not surpass that of Judah"* (Zech. 12:7). The first part was fulfilled by the War of Independence in 1948, when the land of Judah was restored to the Jews (survivors of the tribe of Judah), and the second in 1967 by the Six Day War. God Himself destroyed all the nations that came against Jerusalem: *"And on that day I will seek to destroy all the nations that come against Jerusalem"* (Zech. 12:9).

Furthermore, I also understand that Zechariah 13 speaks about other events that have been already fulfilled, such as the **Nazi Holocaust**, when two-thirds of the Jewish people were cut off and perished: *"In the whole land, declares the LORD, two thirds shall be cut off and perish, and **one third shall be left alive**"* (Zech. 13:8). It is also worth pointing out that a separation of time and event in some of these verses is not unusual in prophecy, especially when we look at Zechariah 13:7, which clearly refers to the moment when Jesus the Shepherd was struck and the sheep scattered: *"Strike the shepherd, and the sheep will be scattered."* Thus, we see a break in subject and time that was recognized by Jesus and quoted by the early Gospel writers (Matt. 26:31 and Mk. 14:27).

Returning to Matthew 24:29-31, we can see that Jesus clarified that certain cataclysmic signs in heaven would be visible before the

Son of Man is to appear in the clouds to raise His elect, very similar to what is described in the Sixth Seal and the subsequent Six Trumpets. But Jesus adds that **before those events**, we should watch the "**fig tree**," which clearly represents Israel. *"From the fig tree learn its lesson: as soon as its branch becomes tender and puts out its leaves, you know that summer is near"* (Matt. 24:32). Metaphorically, Israel will "sprout leaves" and "branch out," ready to produce its "fruit." This is what Revelation 7 is all about. Sometime during the same time in which we see the signs of the Sixth Seal and first Six Trumpets, Israel will be saved. *"So also, **when you see all these things**, you know that **he is near, at the very gates**. Truly, I say to you, this generation will not pass away until all these things take place"* (Matt. 24:33-34). Thus, I believe that **the generation that sees Israel's salvation is the same one that will be raised alive when Jesus appears in the clouds!**

Regarding some objections to the list of names of the sons of Israel in Revelation 7:5-8, which are not quite precise, it seems like John's main purpose was not to be precise but to represent all those in Israel who will be saved (Rom. 11:26), those who are inscribed in the Book of Life (Dan. 12:1). As a community, Israel will confess that Jesus has been, and will always be, their Redeemer and Messiah.

Joel also spoke of this moment of Israel's salvation as occurring **right before** the Lord calls His own. Jews will first "call on the name of the Lord" and be saved, and then they will "escape" His coming wrath when He "calls" them up:

> *"And I will show wonders in the heavens and on the earth, blood and fire and columns of smoke. The sun shall be turned to darkness, and the moon to blood, before the great and awesome day of the LORD comes. And it shall come to pass that **everyone who calls on the name of the LORD***

shall be **saved**. *For in Mount Zion and in Jerusalem there shall be those who* **escape**, *as the LORD has said, and* **among the survivors** *shall be those whom the LORD calls"* (Joel 2:30-32).

The Hebrew word above for "**saved**" is *malat*, which means a deliverance or a leaping out, and the word for "**escape**" is *p'leitah*, as in a rescue, both similar to a resurrection. These Jews that will be raised are *"among the survivors"* of their long season of Great Tribulation. Jesus even alluded to this when He lamented about the hardness of Jerusalem and their long desolation, and stated that His people would not see Him again until they welcomed Him as the One who comes in the name of the Lord. *"See,* **your house is left to you desolate**. *For I tell you, you will not see me again,* **until you say**, *'Blessed is he who comes in the name of the Lord.'"* (Matt. 23:38-39). This also confirms that they will **accept** Him before they **see** Him, not vice-versa!

The fact that Israel receives the *"seal of the living God"* (Rev. 7:2) can be seen as equivalent to when Christians are sealed with the Holy Spirit after being saved. *"And do not grieve the Holy Spirit of God, by whom you were* **sealed for the day of redemption**" (Eph. 4:30). It is the main requirement for being included in the redemption, whether Jew or Christian. God's seal of the Holy Spirit will distinguish His people from all those who will later receive the seal of the Beast. The phrase *"day of redemption"* in Ephesians 4:30 clearly refers to the day of the resurrection of the saints, so the sealing of Israel during the Sixth Seal and first Six Trumpets is in preparation for this transcendental event. The day of the resurrection ("rapture," for some) will only become imminent once **this** has happened. But no one knows the day or the hour, not even the Son. Only the Father really knows, because it is totally in His hands (Matt. 24:36).

This sealing of the 144,000 is also the ultimate fulfillment of God's original purposes for His *kahal* (*ekklesía, as termed in the Septuagint*). At this moment, Jews and Gentiles will truly become one congregation of called-out people. God's "church" or *ekklesía* will become its true and rightful self, a holy union of both Jewish and Gentile people of God, as illustrated by the anticipated heavenly joy and celebration:

> *"After this I looked, and behold, a great multitude that no one could number, **from every nation**, from all tribes and peoples and languages, **standing before the throne and before the Lamb**, clothed in white robes, with palm branches in their hands, and crying out with a loud voice, 'Salvation belongs to our God who sits on the throne, and to the Lamb!'"* (Rev. 7:9-10).

In Revelation 14 there is an even clearer picture of this. The Jewish people will stand on Mount Zion (figuratively speaking) with the Lamb, and they will have the *"Father's name written on their forehead"* (v. 1). It pictures them in heaven, *"singing a new song before the throne"* (v. 3). They will be so pure before God that it will be **as if** they had *"not defiled themselves with women"* (v. 4). This is not meant to be taken literally, because the whole poetic and symbolic description is that of complete union with the Lamb and with other believers in the Messiah. *"...It is these who follow the Lamb wherever he goes. These have been **redeemed from mankind as firstfruits for God and the Lamb**, and in their mouth no lie was found, for they are blameless"* (Rev: 14:4-5).

The Jewish sage Saadia Gaon of the 7th century, in his treatise about the resurrection of the dead, described their resurrection as an event that the majority of Jews understood will occur together with their salvation: "Let me say now that I find that the masses of the children of Israel cherish the belief that the Creator, blessed be He, will bring the dead back to life **at the time of the redemption... at the time of the salvation**."[81]

He adds: "we do not allege that they will come back of their own accord but merely that their Creator will bring them to life. There is no rational objection to the doctrine because the restoration of something that has once existed and disintegrated is more plausible logically than *creatio ex nihilo*...God will bring the dead of His nation to life again **at the time of the redemption**."[82]

Admittedly, this Jewish concept of "salvation" or "redemption" refers to the Messianic Kingdom and does not consider the possibility that they will actually need to admit that Jesus is this long-expected Messiah. But those of us who have already believed in their Messiah and have been grafted into the olive tree, *"and now share in the nourishing root of the olive tree"* (Rom. 11:17), understand that they will eventually believe in Him, and they will again *"be grafted in, for God has the power to graft them in again"* (Rom. 11:23).

> *"And in this way all Israel will be saved, as it is written, 'The Deliverer will come from Zion, he will banish ungodliness from Jacob'...For the gifts and the calling of God are irrevocable"* (Rom. 11:26, 29).

All these declarations imply that their moment of belief will not occur **until they actually see the signs in heaven** and become

---

[81] Saadia Gaon ben Yosef, "Concerning the Resurrection of the Dead in this World" in *The Book of Beliefs and Opinions*, trans. Samuel Rosenblatt (Massachusetts: Yale Press, 1948), 409.

[82] Ibid, 267.

ready for their resurrection! Then they will call upon the name of the Lord and welcome His Messiah. Thus, amidst the cataclysmic heavenly signs, we will see the lifting of the Jewish veil.

Paul spoke about a veil over the hearts of the Jewish people, but when they receive the revelation about the Messiah, their eyes will be spiritually opened and the veil will be lifted.[83] As defended before, this will not happen by forced conversion of the Jews, but they will each receive a direct revelation from the Holy Spirit according to each family, starting with the father, the mother, and then the children.

> "...*For to this day, when they read the old covenant, that same veil remains unlifted, because only through Christ is it taken away...But when one turns to the Lord,* **the veil is removed**" (2 Cor. 3:14, 16).

Another crucial Biblical evidence of the fact that the Jews will believe in *Yeshua* during the sounding of the Trumpets is found in the symbolism for each Feast of the Lord. Each feast described in Leviticus 23 is predictive of what Jesus did or will do in order to save His people. Some people interpret the sound of the trumpet as God's call for Israel to return to their land. This is possible, but it could also represent the moment when Jesus calls His people to repentance in preparation for their imminent resurrection. This sound of the shofar will provoke the Jews to repent and believe in Jesus as the Messiah, which is represented by the Day of Atonement, and then they will see their immediate resurrection. (See Appendix 5.)

Most Christians agree that the Jews will finally believe in Jesus

---

[83] We also read about a "veil" over all the nations, which will be removed at the time of the Messianic Kingdom (Isa. 25:7).

or *Yeshua* as their Messiah, but what is argued about is **when** it will actually happen. A large majority of defenders of all three categories of Premillennialism propose that Jews will not believe until after the "rapture," i.e. during the "Tribulation," or during the Millennium. This formula has been repeated so often that no one even questions it anymore. But as defended previously, the Jews must believe in Jesus **before the resurrection** so they can participate in the eternal Kingdom of God. Their bodies must first become **imperishable by resurrection**, or they could never enter it:

"...*flesh and blood cannot inherit the kingdom of God...*" (1 Cor. 15:50).

3) The Final Seventh Trumpet

It is very important to note that God's people, both Jews and Christians, will still be on earth at the time of the first Six Trumpets. Yet I believe that many could be protected from their disastrous effects. Isn't this what is meant by: "*Come, my people, enter your chambers, and shut your doors behind you;* **hide yourselves for a little while until the fury has passed by**" (Isa. 26:20)? There will be miraculous protection for God's people from the worst of the calamities, as when God protected Israel while living in the land of Goshen. The people were protected from the third to the tenth plagues sent against the Egyptians.

> "*But on that day I will set apart the land of Goshen, where my people dwell, so that no swarms of flies shall be there, that you may know that I am the LORD in the midst of the earth. Thus* **I will put a division between my people and your people**..." (Ex. 8:22-23).

The Israelites were protected from the last seven plagues in order to show God's power and authority above the Egyptian gods, and *"so that you may know that there is none like me in all the earth"* (Ex. 9:14). By this same principle, Christians and Jews may merely witness, though some may experience to a degree, the acts of God meant for unbelievers in vindication of His people during the first Six Trumpets.

A recent sample of what could lie ahead occurred on January 27, 2019, when Cuba was hit by a very large and unusual tornado (not hurricane), killing six people and destroying about 4,000 homes. I received an email from a Christian there who testified that, despite the disaster, no Christians were affected, nor were their churches or properties damaged.

Psalm 17:2 says that our vindication will come from the Lord: *"From your presence let my vindication come! Let your eyes behold the right!"* Would God really subject His righteous saints to the punishment meant in their own vindication? Thus, though it is possible that modern Christians and Jews might experience the effects of worldwide disasters during the "Trumpets," perhaps they will not be as directly affected as the unbelievers. In any case, I believe that when Jesus said that this time would be shortened for the sake of the elect (Mk. 13:20), He was referring to the *"tribulation of those days"* (Matt. 24:29).

But believers must be careful not to neglect their salvation and drift away from the truth while experiencing the *"tribulation of those days."* Contrary to some allegations that Christians cannot lose their salvation, Jesus said that this drifting away is possible: *"And then many will **fall away** and betray one another and hate one another. And many false prophets will arise and lead many **astray"*** (Matt. 24:10-11). This may happen to those whose roots are not sufficiently deep in Jesus and in the rich and pure soil of God's Word, and when tribulation arises they will fall away (Mar. 4:17). Only persevering believers will victoriously escape from the vengeful wrath of God, that is, the future Bowls of

Wrath meant for unbelievers. If they drift away, or are led astray by others, there will be no guarantee of His protection:

> *"Therefore we must pay much closer attention to what we have heard,* **lest we drift away from it**. *For since the message declared by angels proved to be reliable, and every transgression or disobedience received a just retribution,* **how shall we escape** *if we* **neglect** *such a great salvation?"* (Heb. 2:1-3a).

Even though the Antichrist will not yet be able to take over while God's people are on the earth, in a certain sense Satan has nearly overcome the real Church, making it very difficult to preach the Word in many places of the world and having created a "prostituted" and fictitious church. Even in our Western societies, we can see how the Church has defiled itself with divisions, love of power, and fleshly desires, becoming more secular and/or being drawn into the occult and other satanic ideologies, while Islam is quickly gaining a global stronghold. But lacking coherence and a unifying leader, we still do not see the "Man of Lawlessness" that will threaten mankind after we are gone.

Returning to Revelation 3:10 and its mention of the church in Philadelphia about being kept or protected during the "hour of trial," the Greek word for "trial" in that verse is actually *"pirasmós,"* which represents a beneficial discipline of some sort that is divinely permitted. God doesn't want to prevent us from going through certain necessary trials, because He wants to use them as a way of perfecting us. But Peter distinguishes this type of disciplinary correction from actual "punishment" or *"kolazo:"*

> *"…and if he* [God] *rescued righteous Lot, greatly distressed by the sensual conduct of the wicked… then the Lord knows how to* **rescue** *[rhoumai] the godly from* **trials** *[piramsós], and to keep the unrighteous under* **punishment** *[kolazo] until the* **day of judgment"** (2 Pet. 2:7, 9).

The idea here is that God will eventually "rescue" or "deliver" (*rhoumai*) His people from their trials in the same manner that He eventually rescued Lot from the wicked environment of Sodom and Gomorrah, which he withstood for a certain time. God took Lot out of Sodom when the time came to destroy it, and He will protect us while we are in the midst of tribulations [*thlipsis*] and trials [*pirasmós*] until it is time for us to be rescued or delivered, which is right before the unrighteous will experience their punishment [*kolazo*]. These sinners will be kept on earth for their future punishment on the Day of Judgment because they were never resurrected with the believers. The Greek *rhoumai* above is the same as in 1 Thessalonians 1:10, where the believers wait for Jesus, *"who* **delivers us from** *the wrath to come,"* here using *"rhoumai apó"* for delivering us **before** the wrath.

Psalm 50:15 says: *"…call upon me in the day of trouble [***tzarah***]; I will deliver you [***chalatz***], and you shall glorify me."* The word "trouble" (*tzarah*) also means tribulation, but God promised that He would finally deliver (*chalatz*) them, which implies a drawing out or taking away, and then they would glorify Him.

Psalm 50:5 also says: *"Gather [***asaph***] to me my faithful ones, who made a covenant with me by sacrifice!"* In this verse, "gather" (*asaph*) implies a taking up, receiving or assembling together of God's faithful people, similar to *chalatz*, thus a resurrection of those people who live in Covenant with God, which include both Jews and Gentiles. This is very similar to Ezekiel 37, the chapter of Israel's dry bones coming to life, a clear picture of its spiritual and physical resurrection from the dead.

After the symbolic 144,000 Jewish people have been saved (Rev. 14:1-5), we hear the last preaching of the Gospel to all the world, this time proclaimed by angels and not by men (verse 6). It is also a warning to all those who refuse to believe, and includes the things for which they will be later judged at the time of the final judgment. They need to know beforehand what their sentence will be:

> "…*If anyone worships the beast and its image and receives a mark on his forehead or on his hand,* he also will drink the wine of **God's wrath,** poured full strength into the cup of his anger, and he will be **tormented with fire and sulfur** in the presence of the holy angels and in the presence of the Lamb'" (Rev. 14:7-10).

Whatever the mark of the beast will be, they will somehow carry a spiritual distinction that identifies them as belonging to Satan, rather than to God. And God's punishment or *kolazo* against sinners will be totally justified, because those people will have proven to have impenitent hearts.

> "But because of your **hard and impenitent heart** you are **storing up wrath for yourself on the day of wrath** when God's righteous judgment will be revealed….for those who are self-seeking and do not obey the truth, but obey unrighteousness, there will be **wrath and fury**" (Rom. 2:5-8).

Yet, the section of Revelation 14 is also followed by a clear message to **believers**, which proves that this actually belongs to the time of the tribulations before the resurrection. Christians may be feeling the initial effects of the spirit of the Antichrist, but are exhorted to endure until the end: *"Here is a call for the **endurance of the saints**, those who keep the commandments of God and their faith in Jesus"* (Rev. 14:12). It is a word of comfort regarding the martyrs and other Christians who die in Christ, because they will be eternally blessed: *"'...**Blessed are the dead who die in the Lord** from now on.' 'Blessed indeed,' says the Spirit, 'that they may rest from their labors, for their deeds follow them!'"* (Rev. 14:13). Thus, the first Six Trumpets are not meant to threaten God's people, but to give them hope regarding their imminent resurrection and reunion with Christ. The Biblical principle is that these trumpet sounds are a reminder to God to save His people (Num. 10:10). The announcement of the trumpets come first, and then God displays His salvation!

And right before the last and Seventh Trumpet is to be sounded, and when Jesus receives the order to put in His sickle for the harvest in Revelation 14:14-16, Jesus will appear in the clouds to gather up His people at the "loud trumpet call" of the angels (Matt. 24:31). God will give His heavenly shout to ***"Come up here!"*** (Rev. 11:12-15). Paul describes this as the "last trumpet" (1 Cor. 15:52), or merely as the "sound of a trumpet" (1 Thess. 4:16). Sadly, I am often puzzled as to why so many Christian teachers and theologians refuse to relate Revelation 11:12 with the desired resurrection of God's people. Since their own preconceived expectation is so firm in their minds, they do not recognize this as the climatic event that both Christians and Jews have been longing for during centuries.

When Jesus said that He would not ask the Father to **take us out of** (*"airo ek"*) the hour of trial, but that He would ask the Father to **keep us from** (*"tereo ek"*) the evil one (Jn. 17:15), He was referring to His guarding and protecting us in the midst of tribulations. But "*airo ek*" is exactly what the resurrection will be like before the last Trumpet sounds, a "lifting out." Jesus said that He looked forward to the day when we would be with ("*metá*") Him where He is: *"Father, I desire that they also, whom you have given me, **may be with me where I am**, to see my glory that you have given me…"* (Jn. 17:24).

Pretribulationists such as Walvoord do not think that this can refer to the "rapture" or resurrection because the whole world will be watching it.[84] They allege for some reason that it needs to be a secret event, and they willfully ignore what Jesus said in Matthew 24:30, that states: *"all the tribes of the earth will mourn, and **they will see the Son of Man** coming on the clouds of heaven with power and great glory."* Because of that, Walvoord simply associates this moment with the ascension of Jesus on the Mount of Olives in Acts 1. But Jesus also said: *"For **as the lightning comes from the east and shines as far as the west**, so will be the coming of the Son of Man. Wherever the corpse is, there the vultures will gather"* (Matt. 24:27-28). By this He meant that His coming would be as evident to all as the lightning that stretches in the sky from east to west and as the circle of vultures above a corpse.

In contrast, Ladd did see a connection between Revelation 11:12 and a resurrection, but since he still interpreted the two witnesses as two real people, he only considered it to be the "ascension" of **these two specific people**, not the resurrection of the whole body of believers.[85] Many others only see this as the moment of the resurrection of the **Christian martyrs during the tribulation period**. This is the trouble with being too literal in their reading of the apocalyptic book of Revelation, the divinely-inspired apocalyptic book *par excellence*.

---

[84] Walvoord, *Revelation*, 184.

[85] George E. Ladd, *A Commentary on the Revelation of John* (Grand Rapids, MI: Eerdmans, 1972), 159.

Payne acknowledged that most people interpret the two witnesses as two specific people, whether Moses and Elijah, Zerubbabel and Joshua, or some other prophets. But he also understood how they could be interpreted to symbolize **all believers**: "Since the resurrection and heavenward ascension of the two witnesses corresponds to the actual experience of the dead in Christ, rising at His shout and at the sounding of the last trumpet…it seems proper to identify the witnesses with all believers who have died, too often slain for their proclamation of God's word, the law and the prophets."[86] Nevertheless, he interpreted that the resurrection of the saints will occur at the same moment as Jesus' triumphant return to establish His Kingdom, and that the marriage supper will be celebrated later in the earthly Kingdom: "…the raising and rapture of the two witnesses (11:11-12) occurs in the same hour as the great earthquake and the conversion of the Jews at Christ's triumphant return; the marriage supper of the Lamb…occurs just after the Lord has taken up His reign on earth."[87] Thus, his thesis was that, since John does not use the term resurrection in reference to this event, as he clearly mentioned it in Revelation 20, "it would appear unwarranted to postulate an earlier resurrection for 'the other groups' of the church."[88]

But how does Revelation 11:12 negate the great resurrection moment merely because the word does not appear there? Jesus never used the term in Matthew 24, nor did Paul use it in 1 Thessalonians 4. How about all the other Old Testament texts that describe the resurrection of the dead without using the term? Isn't the description of the event enough to have us recognize it as such? After all, both Jesus and Paul described the Trumpet as being one of the main

---

[86] Payne, 617.

[87] Ibid, 618.

[88] Ibid.

elements of the resurrection, as we also read here: *"Then **the seventh angel blew his trumpet**, and there were loud voices in heaven, saying, 'The kingdom of the world has become the kingdom of our Lord and of his Christ, and he shall reign forever and ever'"* (Rev. 11:15).

Right before this, God's voice will thunder from heaven: *"Come up here!"* or in Greek: ἀνάβητε ὧδε *(anábente ode)*, or in Hebrew: עלו הנה *(alú hineh)*, or in any of all the languages of the world! Whichever language He uses, all believers will understand and rise to meet the Lamb in the air, as an eager Bride goes forth at the arrival of her bridegroom to enter her *"chuppah"* with Him.

In the duplicated narration of Revelation 14 we also see another illustration of the moment of the resurrection, both of the saints as of the wicked, but presented in a different way. In Revelation 14, we read that an angel (presumably at the Father's indication) made the call for Jesus to play His part in the event:

> *"Then I looked, and behold, a white cloud, and seated on the cloud one like a **son of man** [Jesus], with a golden crown on his head, and a sharp sickle in his hand. And another **angel** came out of the temple, calling with a loud voice to him who sat on the cloud, '**Put in your sickle, and reap**, for the hour to reap has come, for the harvest of the earth is fully ripe.' So **he who sat on the cloud** [Jesus] swung his sickle across the earth, and **the earth was reaped**"* (Rev. 14:14-16).

It is important to reemphasize that, after this point, it will be impossible for anyone to truly believe and be saved. First of all, Jesus said that the door would be "closed" after He takes His bride to the marriage feast: *"...the bridegroom came, and those who were ready went in with him to the marriage feast, and **the door was shut**"* (Matt. 25:10).

Also, their own rebellion will have caused them to shut their hearts and minds because they rejected His Messiah when they had the opportunity to do so. Even though many nowadays do not interpret Jesus' words in Matthew 24:37-42 as a reference to this event, it clearly says that *"…two men will be in the field; one will be **taken** and one left. Two women will be grinding at the mill; one will be **taken** and one left"* (Matt. 24:40-41). Just like in the days of Noah, those that are not taken up [*paralambano*] at that unique moment will remain behind and will be swept away by the wrath of God.

F. Mystery of God Fulfilled

1) Marriage Supper of the Lamb in Heaven

We read in Revelation 10:7 that *"in the days of the trumpet call to be sounded by the seventh angel, the **mystery of God would be fulfilled**, just as he announced to his servants the prophets."* And in chapter 11 we read about what will happen both **in heaven** and **on earth** concurrently at the moment of the resurrection of the saints. In heaven, loud voices will cry: *"The kingdom of the world has become the kingdom of our Lord and of his Christ, and he shall reign forever and ever* (v. 15),*"* while on earth, *"their enemies watched them"* (v. 12) and *"the nations raged"* (v. 18). In heaven, God's temple will be opened and the Ark of the Covenant will be seen inside (v. 19), while on earth, there will be a great earthquake killing 7,000 people, and one tenth of Jerusalem will fall (v. 13). Even though it says that they will give *"glory to the God of heaven,"* they will not actually repent (Rev. 9:20-21; 16:9-11). They will simply acknowledge that all of those events are really proceeding from God.

Chapters 15-16 also narrate the events that will occur in heaven at the same time that the seven angels prepare to pour out the last seven plagues of the Bowls of Wrath on earth. We read about the beautiful sea of glass and the song that the redeemed of God will sing: *"And they sing the **song of Moses**, the servant of God, and the **song of the Lamb**, saying, "Great and amazing are your deeds, O Lord God the Almighty! Just and true are your ways, O King of the nations!"* (Rev. 15:3). This reflects the perfect fulfillment of the *"one new man"* in Ephesians 2:15, a perfect blending of the Jewish and Gentile believers in the Messiah as we sing the song of Moses, as well as the song of the Lamb. Meanwhile on earth, the unbelievers will experience the tyrannical domination of the Second Beast from the Earth and almost immediately the Bowls of Wrath.

Chapter 19 offers a more detailed description of the saints in heaven, when all the resurrected believers will be eternally wedded to our Messiah and will be celebrating together the "Marriage Supper of the Lamb."

"...Then I heard what seemed to be the voice of a great multitude, like the roar of many waters and like the sound of mighty peals of thunder, crying out, 'Hallelujah! For the Lord our God the Almighty reigns. Let us rejoice and exult and give him the glory, for the marriage of the Lamb has come, and his Bride has made herself ready; it was granted her to clothe herself with fine linen, bright and pure" - for the fine linen is the righteous deeds of the saints"' (Rev. 19:5-8).

Do we ever wonder why God makes such a big deal about a marriage covenant? For God, the state of marriage is the holiest and most intimate type of relationship ever to be had. He made a marriage covenant with Israel on Mount Sinai when He gave them the Law on tablets of stone, and He betrothed the Jewish people to Himself forever. This was not purely symbolic, but in earnest. He told Israel: *"And I will betroth you to me forever. I will betroth you to me **in righteousness and in justice, in steadfast love and in mercy.***

*I will betroth you to me **in faithfulness**. And you shall know the LORD"* (Hosea 2:19-20). And once betrothed, the bride was considered as good as married: *"For your Maker is **your husband**, the LORD of hosts is his name; and the Holy One of Israel is your Redeemer, the God of the whole earth he is called"* (Isa. 54:5).

God expected Israel to be faithful to Him as He would be to them, but later descendants broke the covenant that God had made with their forefathers (Jer. 11:10). God then made a New Covenant with Israel, and this time it was different.

> *"For this is the covenant that I will make with the house of Israel after those days, declares the LORD: I will put my law within them, and **I will write it on their hearts**. And I will be their God, and they shall be my people"* (Jer. 31:33).

This New Covenant would not just be written on stone, but in their hearts. It would also now include all people who are willing to enter into this intimate relationship with God through His Son: *"...I will give you* [Jesus] *as a **covenant for the people, a light for the nations**..."* (Isa. 42:6-7). So God paid the price of redemption through the blood of His divine Son (the human image of God) for all those who would call upon His Name.

And we see this same love of God expressed in the New Testament through Jesus' love for His "bride," which is not limited merely to the Church, as many Christians think. Our God is not an adulterous God, nor does He have two wives, so this means that **His one and only "bride"** is really a spiritual body that consists of **all saints, true Jews and Christians** who have been redeemed by the blood of His Son. The Apostle Paul said *"this mystery is profound, and I am saying that it refers to Christ and the church"* (Eph. 5:32).

God's love is also impressive when we consider that He included a whole book in the Bible dealing only with this type of courtship, betrothal, and joyful marriage. *"Set me as a **seal upon your heart**, as a seal upon your arm, for love is strong as death, jealousy is fierce as the grave…Many waters cannot quench love, neither can floods drown it"* (Song of Sol. 8:6-7).

God is such a profound romantic! His love for His bride, both Israel and the Church, has been His main focus ever since He created mankind and sought to have a true relationship with us. Our romantic bridegroom, our Messiah and Lamb, will rejoice over His spiritual bride with great love:

> *"…**I have loved you with an everlasting love**; therefore I have continued my faithfulness to you. Again I will build you, and you shall be built, O virgin Israel! Again you shall adorn yourself with tambourines and shall go forth in the dance of the merrymakers"* (Jer. 31:3-4).

> *"…**as the bridegroom rejoices over the bride**, so shall your God rejoice over you"* (Isa. 62:5).

> *"You have **captivated my heart, my sister, my bride**; you have captivated my heart with one glance of your eyes, with one jewel of your necklace"* (Song of Solomon 4:9).

> *"**How beautiful is your love, my sister, my bride**! How much better is your love than wine, and the fragrance of your oils than any spice!"* (Song of Solomon 4:10).

> *"The LORD your God is in your midst, a mighty one who will save; he will rejoice over you with gladness; **he will quiet**

you by his love; *he will exult over you with loud singing"* (Zeph. 3:17).

2) Second Beast's Dominion on Earth

In stark contrast to this beautiful heavenly scene following the resurrection of the saints, the 24 elders announce the beginning of the end for non-believers. They offer a prayer of thanksgiving before describing the final picture of Christ's reign, God's wrath, the judgment of the unrighteous, the rewarding of God's servants, and the destruction of the destroyers.

> *"We give thanks to you, Lord God Almighty, who is and who was, for you have taken your great power and begun to **reign**. The nations raged, but your **wrath** came, and the time for the dead to be **judged**, and for **rewarding** your servants, the prophets and saints, and those who fear your name, both small and great, and for **destroying the destroyers** of the earth"* (Rev. 11:17-18).

Chapters 17 and 18 describe how things will be on earth under the dictatorship of the Antichrist, including his repudiation and destruction of the prostituted Church before finally being punished by God. This Second Beast from the Earth, which will have two horns like a lamb but speak like a dragon, will force people to worship the First Beast of the Sea, *"whose mortal wound was healed"* (Rev. 13:12). He will be performing great signs and miracles so as to downplay Jesus' own signs and miracles, and he will present himself as even greater than Jesus. He will give "new life" to the ancient Muslim Ottoman Empire, at this time probably a joint Sunni and Shiite

Caliphate, together with the United Nations, the European Union, plus the Vatican, and will force people to submit to this government upon threat of death (Rev. 13:15). All people remaining after the resurrection will be forced to have the Antichrist's mark:

> *"Also it causes all, both small and great, both rich and poor, both free and slave, to be marked on the right hand or the forehead, so that no one can buy or sell unless he has the mark, that is, the name of the beast or the number of its name"* (Rev. 13:16-17).

Chapters 17 to 18 provide more details as to how this Caliphate will look like, including a description of the "Harlot" who has been riding on the back of the Beast (Rev. 17:3). I believe that this Harlot represents the historically sacrilegious Roman Catholic Vatican and the modern "Christians" who joined Islam under the banner of "Chrislam," because the Beast will eventually hate her, make her desolate, devour her, and burn her up with fire. *"For God has put it into their hearts to carry out his purpose by being of one mind and handing over their royal power to the beast, until the words of God are fulfilled"* (Rev. 17:17).

This Satanic kingdom could last for *"a little while"* (17:10) or for *"one hour"* (17:12; 18:10; 18:17; 18:19), whatever that means precisely. It will be sufficient time for the Second Beast that *"was, and is not, and is about to rise from the bottomless pit and go to destruction"* (Rev. 17:8) to believe that he has finally obtained his goal of controlling the world, and then to annihilate the Harlot who was *"drunk with the blood of the saints, the blood of the martyrs of Jesus"* (Rev. 17:6).

Because of these coming judgments upon the Harlot, God has been warning His people, real Christians who might be under the deception of the Vatican and the Roman Catholic Church, to *"come out of her"* while they still have the chance (before the resurrection) so that they do not participate in her sins and thus receive her plagues (Rev. 18:4). Besides her wealth through trade with foreign governments, she got rich off the human slave trade (Rev. 18:13) and immorality (Rev. 18:9). *"And in her was found the blood of prophets and of saints, and of all who have been slain on earth"* (Rev. 18:24). God also tells His people to **rejoice because this Harlot will be judged**: *"Rejoice over her, O heaven, and you saints and apostles and prophets, for God has given judgment for you against her!"* (Rev. 18:20).

Revelation 16 describes the first four "bowls" of God's Wrath upon: (1) the earth, (2) the sea, (3) the rivers and springs, and (4) the sun. Then the Fifth Bowl will be poured out upon the throne of the Beast, who will blaspheme God but will not repent. The Sixth Bowl will be poured out upon the Euphrates River, which will dry up and allow the kings from the east and from all over the world to join the Dragon (Satan), the Beast (the worldwide Islamic Caliphate), and the False Prophet (Mohammad's Mahdi) for making war against the Lamb in *Har Megiddo* (Armageddon). The Seventh Bowl will bring such terrible earthquakes as never before, where islands disappear and mountains fall away (Rev. 16:20). It ends by God pouring out His fearful wrath (*thumós*). *"...The seventh angel poured out his bowl into the air, and a loud voice came out of the temple, from the throne, saying, 'It is done!'"*

The prophet Zephaniah also announced this terrible day of wrath, distress, and anguish against those who had sinned against God.

> *"The great day of the LORD is near, near and hastening fast; the sound of the day of the LORD is bitter; the mighty man cries aloud there. A **day of wrath** is that day, a day of **distress and anguish**, a day of **ruin and devastation,** a day of **darkness and gloom**, a day of **clouds and thick darkness**, a day of trumpet blast*

*and battle cry against the fortified cities and against the lofty battlements. I will bring **distress on mankind,** so that they shall walk like the blind, because they have sinned against the LORD…"* (Zeph. 1:14-17).

I will not enter into more details here, since it does not really affect the dilemma of when the Messiah will come for His people in relation to the "Tribulation." Suffice it to say that Christians will not experience these dreadful Bowls of Wrath, nor do I expect that once we are in heaven with our Messiah we will be able to see what is happening on earth. Our ecstatic joy might be quenched if we saw their extreme suffering. But we will be totally immersed in our loving and just Savior and Redeemer, knowing that He did everything possible to give everyone the same opportunity to believe in Him and to accept Him as we had.

G. Christ's Return and Final Events

1) *Parousía* and Messianic Kingdom

Once the Marriage Supper of the Lamb has been celebrated and the Bowls of God's Wrath (*thumós*) have been poured out on all the remaining inhabitants on earth, Jesus prepares Himself for the battle that has been brewing in chapter 16 in order to finally establish His Kingdom. He is the "Faithful and True" One who leads His army of angels and resurrected believers on white horses. *"From his mouth comes a sharp sword with which to strike down the nations, and he will rule them with a rod of iron…"* (Rev. 19:15).

We read in Revelation 16:12-17 that the survivors among the nations begin to gather for the **Battle at Armageddon**. *"And I* saw the beast and the kings of the earth with their armies gathered to make war against him who was sitting on the horse and against his army" (Rev. 19:19). But the Messiah's army will be far more superior, before whom they cannot stand:

> "Behold, the Lord comes **with ten thousands of his holy ones**, to execute judgment on all and to convict all the ungodly of all their deeds of ungodliness that they have committed in such an ungodly way, and of all the harsh things that ungodly sinners have spoken against him" (Jude 1:14-15).

When Jesus arrives, Jerusalem will be *"split **into three parts**, and the cities of the nations"* will fall (Rev. 16:19). Zechariah says that Jerusalem will be split into **two** parts, but that difference is unimportant. Again, numbers are mainly general descriptions or symbolisms.

> "On that day his feet shall **stand on the Mount of Olives** that lies before Jerusalem on the east, and the Mount of Olives shall be **split in two** from east to west by a very wide valley, so that one half of the Mount shall move northward, and the other half southward" (Zech. 14:4).

The importance is that these unrepentant people will be *"slain by the sword that came from the mouth of him who was sitting on the horse, and all the birds were gorged with their flesh"* (Rev. 19:21).

Paul confirmed to the Thessalonians that God would afflict those who afflicted them when Jesus returns with His mighty angels to inflict vengeance and to be glorified in His saints in order to establish His Kingdom:

"This is evidence of the righteous judgment of God, that you may be considered worthy of the kingdom of God, for which you are also suffering— since indeed God considers it just to **repay with affliction those who afflict you**, *and to grant relief to you who are afflicted as well as to us, when the* **Lord Jesus is revealed from heaven with his mighty angels** *in flaming fire, inflicting vengeance on those who do not know God and on those who do not obey the gospel of our Lord Jesus"* (2 Thess. 1:5-8).

In Revelation 14:17-20, we also read about this moment when Jesus will return to establish the Millennial Kingdom. Verses 14-16 describe the first "harvest," or the day of resurrection of the saints, when Jesus would swing His sickle to gather His holy people. But that will be followed by another "harvest," this time done by an angel, who could be called the "grim reaper":

"...So **the angel swung his sickle** *across the earth and gathered the grape harvest of the earth and* **threw it into the great winepress of the wrath of God**. *And the winepress was trodden outside the city, and blood flowed from the winepress, as high as a horse's bridle, for 1,600 stadia"* (Rev. 14:18-20).

This is in reference to Armageddon, which represents the defeat of the *"armies gathered to make war against him who was sitting on the horse and against his army"* (Rev. 19:19). *"From his mouth comes a sharp sword with which to strike down the nations, and he will rule them with a rod of iron. He will tread the winepress of the fury of the wrath of God the Almighty"* (v. 15). Satan will be bound for one thousand years (Rev. 20:2), and the

Beast, along with the False Prophet, will be *"thrown alive into the lake of fire that burns with sulfur"* (Rev. 19:20).

This is the same Kingdom described in Daniel 7:27:

> *"And the kingdom and the dominion and the greatness of the kingdoms under the whole heaven shall be given **to the people of the saints of the Most High**; his kingdom shall be an everlasting kingdom, and all dominions shall serve and obey him."*

2) Second Resurrection, Final Judgment, and Father's Kingdom

At the end of the thousand-year reign or Millennium, we read about the second resurrection of the unrighteous and their final judgment. The great battle described in Revelation 20, which is termed the War of **Gog and Magog,** seems much more similar to the apocalyptic battles of Ezekiel 38-39, and will take place **after the Millennium**, not before. Satan will be released again (Rev. 20:7), and God will bring Gog and other leaders from the far north:

> *"Thus says the Lord GOD: 'On that day, thoughts will come into your mind, and you will devise an evil scheme and say, "I will go up against the land of **unwalled villages**. I will fall upon the quiet people who dwell securely, all of them dwelling without walls, and **having no bars or gates**... You will come up against my people Israel, like a cloud covering the land. **In the latter days** I will bring you against my land, that the nations may know me, when through you, O Gog, I vindicate my holiness before their eyes"* (Ezek. 38:10-11,16).

Even though Ezekiel 39:12 mentions the feast of dead bodies for the birds and the beasts as in Revelation 19:17-18, which describes this to happen at the end of the War of **Armageddon** (the "great supper of God"), Revelation 20 does not mention that after the war of God and Magog. But Revelation 20 does describe God destroying Gog and Magog with fire (Rev. 20:10), as does Ezekiel. In any case, both battles before and after the Millennium seem to be very similar.

"With pestilence and bloodshed I will enter into judgment with him, and I will rain upon him and his hordes and the many peoples who are with him **torrential rains and hailstones, fire and sulfur** *"* (Ezek. 38:22).

The main difference between the narrations of the War of Armageddon and the War of Gog and Magog is that the Beast and the False Prophet will receive their punishment in the lake of fire **before** the Millennium, while the Devil won't be thrown into the lake of fire until **after** the Millennium.

Regarding the Final Judgment at the end of the Millennium, Jesus illustrated this in the parable of Matthew 13:24-43, known in the KJV as the parable of the "wheat and the tares." (The ESV uses the term "weeds" rather than "tares.") I believe that this parable describes the harvest of the "tares" or unbelievers **before** the wheat because it is referring to the time at the end of the Millennium. The reaping of the "tares," or the second resurrection of the unbelievers, will be at the time of the Final Judgment: *"...The harvest is the* **end of the age**, *and the reapers are angels. Just as the weeds are gathered and burned with fire, so will it be at the end of the age..."* (Matt. 13:39-40). These **sons of the devil** will be harvested and burned with fire at the end of the age, and then the **sons of the kingdom** will shine in the Father's eternal Kingdom.

This is a reference to the new heavens and new earth that the Father will make for all those who will live eternally with Him, who had participated in the first resurrection. At this moment, God also refers to the **New Jerusalem** as His bride: *"Come, I will show you the Bride, the wife of the Lamb"* (Rev. 21:9). This is because His bride (redeemed Jewish and Christian believers) and the city are joined together with Him in one united spiritual entity. Thus, the wife of the Lamb or of God will be a group of people living **with Him,** in His own city, in total spiritual unity with God and with each other.

8

Proposed Final Picture of the Puzzle

After placing the various confusing pieces of the final-day scenario puzzle within the non-negotiable and irrefutable framework of God's intended purposes for all mankind, we end up with a general Post-Great Tribulation / Pre-Wrath "Rapture" or Resurrection picture that, according to my estimation, seems more Biblical than any other. Nevertheless, I prefer to call this a **Joint Christian and Jewish Postribulational Pre-Wrath Resurrection** theory. Both eschatologies are on a convergent path towards the same finality, which is a common resurrection of the saints at the end of their earthly tribulations, but before God rains down His wrath upon unrepentant mankind.

The main preoccupation of this book has been to analyze and compare the theories regarding the resurrection of the saints *vis-à-vis* the "tribulation," whether it will be before, in the middle, or at the end of that period. I have proposed a different theory that encompasses a chronology of events that I believe is more in accordance with the entire revealed Word of God, rejecting some of the elements from each theory, but accepting others.

From a **negative** perspective, I avoid a literal and (I believe) erroneous reading of Daniel's last week and the timing elements of

Revelation. Thus, it also excludes: 1) the Pretribulationist concept of the "rapture" of only the Church; 2) the Midtribulationist view of the Sixth Seal as being the mid-point moment for the "rapture" or resurrection of the saints; and 3) the Postribulationist synchronicity of Jesus' return for His saints and with His saints, among many other things. Those pieces do not seem to fit within the theological constraints of Scripture, and when forced to fit, they produce a picture that is outside of any true Biblical scenario.

From a **positive** perspective, some elements that I believe are correct in each of the three typical Pre-, Mid-, and Post- Tribulation theories, and which I include in my theory, are: 1) Christ will come **for** His saints at the moment of the resurrection as a distinct event from when He returns in glory **with** His saints at the second coming or *Parousia*, plus the global dominance of the "Antichrist" between these two events (typical of Pretribulationism); 2) the outpouring of the God's wrath only upon unbelievers following the "tribulation" and "rapture" of the saints (typical of Midtribulationism); and 3) the appearance of Christ "**after** the tribulation of those days" (typical of Postribulationism).

If we use **the Gospels** and the **Apostolic Epistles** as our sole reference for understanding the timing of the last days, Jesus clearly spoke about an extended period of time when there would be wars, famines, and earthquakes in many places, which He described as merely the beginning of birth pains (Matt. 24:6-8). He described an especially intense period of "great tribulation" when He spoke about the destruction of the Temple and the dispersion of the Jewish people (Matt. 24:15-20; Lk. 21:20-24). I understand that this term of "Great Tribulation" is only applicable to that shattering historic event that began in AD 70 to the Jews, including their subsequent dispersion, until the rebirthing of the nation of Israel in 1948. But that "great tribulation" already lies in our past. That was the precise context when Jesus clarified: *"For **then** there will be great tribulation, such as has not been from the beginning of the world until now, no, and never will be"* (Matt. 24:21), very similar to Daniel 12:1, implying that there would be a longer time after that, but not quite as bad. He also emphasized that Christians would be suffering tribulation and death for His name's sake during the same time (Matt. 24:9). And **after** lawlessness has been increased and the love of many has grown cold, **and** the gospel has been proclaimed throughout the whole world, *"**then** the end will come"* (Matt. 24:14). Verse 13 adds the admonition: *"But the one who **endures to the end** will be saved."* All of this indicates an imprecise extended period of time, not just seven short years.

Jesus also warned that Christians could get confused when people declared that He had returned, and that false prophets and antichrists would appear as part of the preparation for the coming of the Antichrist. Muhammad clearly fits the bill here, leading to a religion that supplants Christ, while taking over the land of Israel and the Temple Mount. Islam in evidently Satan's tool to destroy both Judaism and Christianity in direct opposition to God, though it is partially contained at the moment. So when the time approaches for Jesus to gather His saints, which only the Father knows, it will be *"**immediately after the tribulation of those days**"* (Matt. 24:29) most probably referring to the clear divine signs in heaven and on earth that will announce Jesus' appearance.

Jude 1:18 describes what the last days will look like: *"In the last time there will be scoffers, following their own **ungodly passions**. It is these who cause divisions, worldly people, **devoid of the Spirit**."* Even though we can probably say this about every generation, it is definitely truest today. At the right moment, the Jews will welcome their Messiah (Matt. 23:39), and then He will suddenly appear in heaven with His angels and at the sound of a trumpet to gather all His elect together (1 Thess. 4:16-17). He will not yet come down to earth. Once the resurrected saints have acquired new and immortal bodies (1 Cor. 15:53), they will celebrate the marriage supper of the Lamb in heaven (Eph. 5:27) during which time the "Man of Lawlessness" takes over the world (2 Thess. 2:8-12). God will then pour out His wrath upon the remaining people on earth, the "sons of disobedience" who determined not to believe in His Son (Eph. 5:6). This time of wrath is not what Jesus meant as "tribulations," since His description of tribulations and afflictions are what righteous people of God must suffer for God's cause (Phil. 1:29), evil acts done by men under Satan's influence, though these are also allowed or promoted by a just and omnipotent God (2 Cor. 4:17).

After that, Jesus will return to earth with His saints and His angels to put down all rebellion, and He will establish the Messianic Millennial Kingdom (Jude 1:14-16). Jesus the Messiah "...*must reign until He has put all His enemies under His feet. The last enemy that will be abolished is death*" (1 Cor. 15:25-26). He will set His saints on thrones (Matt. 19:28), who will reign with Him for 1,000 years, at the end of which time God will send angelic reapers to raise all the unbelieving dead at the Second Resurrection for their final judgment and punishment (Matt. 13:41-42). *"Then comes the end, when He hands over the* **kingdom to the God and Father***, when He has abolished all rule and all authority and power"* (v. 24). The righteous will shine forever in the Kingdom of their Father (Matt. 13:43).

Using exclusively the book of **Revelation** as our source, I understand that we have been experiencing an extended period of tribulation for almost 2,000 years up to this day, as illustrated by the **first Five Seals** of Revelation 6:1-11. I also interpret that the events of the **Sixth Seal** are merely signs in heaven and on earth as a forewarning of what is to come (Rev. 6:12-17). The **Seventh Seal** contains the **Seven Trumpets** (Rev. 8 and 9), which are also a warning to unbelievers and permitted by God in vindication for what the saints have had to endure. It is very possible that we are already seeing some of the effects of the Seventh Seal since World War II and Israel's return to its land in 1948, if we don't try to be too literal with the text. Sometime during these **signs**, Israel will believe in its Messiah and be sealed with the seal of God (Rev. 7). But before the **Seventh Trumpet** sounds, the **saints will be raised** (Rev. 11:12-19). The **Bowls of Wrath** that follow (Rev. 16) represent God's retribution against evil mankind, in fulfillment of His warnings and in vindication for the suffering of His saints. The redeemed will be enjoying the Marriage Supper of the Lamb (Rev. 19:1-9) during the Second Beast's reign (Rev. 17 and 18) and the later time of the Bowls of Wrath. They will then return with Christ to establish His **Millennial Kingdom** (Rev. 19:11-21). After His victory at **Armageddon**, the Beast and False Prophet will be cast alive into the lake of fire (Rev. 19:20), but Satan will only be bound up for 1,000 years (Rev. 20:2). At the end of the Millennium, the unsaved humanity will come against Jesus and His people for the war of **Gog and Magog**, but fire will come down from heaven and consume them (Rev. 20:9). Then God will throw Satan into the same lake of fire (Rev. 20:10), and raise all the unbelievers in a second resurrection, who will stand before the great throne of judgment. Their names will not appear in the Book of Life, so they will also be cast into the lake of fire (Rev. 20:11-15). Death and Hades will go with them.

Of fundamental importance is the declaration in 1 Corinthians 15:50 in that neither Jews nor Christians can inherit the Kingdom of God without first experiencing the resurrection: *"Now I say this, brethren, that flesh and blood cannot inherit the kingdom of God, nor does the perishable inherit the imperishable.*" This is an event that both faiths look forward to, and expect to participate in, as part of their eschatology, but only after experiencing the resurrection **together**. Clearly, there will be only one unique resurrection event in human history, and both have to experience it at the same time! Yet very few theologians have come to this conclusion since it can be highly controversial, both from the Jewish point of view as well as from the Christian. But if both faiths concur in the basic idea of a coming resurrection and a future Messianic Kingdom, then we must also concur that the resurrection will take place for both at once. There are not two different Messiahs, and there cannot be two separate resurrections or two Kingdoms, just as there are not two separate "brides."

As stated above, since this picture does not follow the typical characteristics of either Pre-, Mid-, or Post- Tribulation, I have termed it a **Joint Christian and Jewish Resurrection Theory,** following the constraints of the corners, edges, and centerpiece of the eschatological puzzle previously defined. I must immediately clarify that this is not an idea that I have been able to find in the writings of any theologian, as diverse as they are, but rather in the Bible texts themselves, trying to be as honest as possible to the whole counsel of God from Genesis to Revelation. God makes sense, and His eschatology also has to make sense.

But we are told to be **patient** for the fulfillment of all things, and **diligent** in serving Him while we wait, as Peter said: *"Therefore, beloved, since you are waiting for these* [events], *be diligent to be found by him without spot or blemish, and at peace"* (2 Pet. 3:14). We should also be diligent in **discerning correct Biblical eschatology**, which *"the ignorant and unstable twist to their own destruction, as they do the other*

Scriptures." Therefore, *"...take care that you are not carried away with the error of lawless people and lose your own stability"* (2 Pet. 3:16-17).

That is why we must seriously inspect everything that is being taught, especially the popular "Pretribulational rapture" theory, which purports to give a "Tribulation-free" pass to Christians, leaving the Jews behind. Jews and Christians have already been suffering for almost two millennia, but we must continue to **wait** and **grow** in grace and knowledge of our Lord, **hastening the day of His return** (2 Pet. 3:12).

Most important of all, any picture that does not have the Jewish and Gentile people of God together as the Body of the Messiah before and during the resurrection must be erroneous, and we might even classify it as a profanation of God's holy masterpiece.

9

Common Eschatological Perspectives in Christianity and Judaism

As part of my conclusions in the defense of this theory, I want to highlight a series of eschatological perspectives that Christianity shares with Judaism. These are important to understand, since this also evidences that there can only be one resurrection that includes both Christians and Jews together. This should not be shocking at all, since our Christian perspective is based on the same Jewish Scriptural source, the one and true Word of God.

a. Messiah ben Joseph and Messiah ben David

The *Babylonian Talmud*, written in the 6th century A.D., has many interesting references regarding the ancient idea of a *ben* (son of) Joseph and a *ben* (son of) David.[89] This text in the *Talmud* makes an association between two "Messiahs" and Zechariah 12:10 regarding their *"mourning"* when they shall look on *"him whom they have pierced."* The text comments: "What is the cause of the mourning? ... One

---

[89] Sukkah 52a

explained, 'The cause is the slaying of Messiah the son of Joseph,' and the other explained, 'The cause is the slaying of the Evil Inclination.'" Further on, it comments: "Our Rabbis taught: the Holy One, blessed be He, will say to the Messiah, the son of David… 'Ask of me anything, and I will give it to thee…' But when he will see that the Messiah, the son of Joseph, is slain, he will say to Him: 'Lord of the Universe, I ask of Thee only the gift of life.'" Even though there is no identification here with Jesus as being both the son of Joseph and David, the fact that the first Messiah was killed, and the second Messiah asked God to give him life is very interesting.

Saadia Gaon also described what early "forebears" described as a series of events that would occur to this son of Joseph: a man will appear in the Upper Galilee "among the descendants of Joseph," around whom there will gather individuals from the Jewish nation.[90] Another man named Armilus will wage war against them and conquer them and the city of Jerusalem, massacring, capturing, and disgracing them. The *descendant of Joseph* will also die. There will then arise a time of great misfortunes, driving them all to the wilderness. As a result, many of them will desert their faith, and only the purified will remain. To those, "Elijah the Prophet" will manifest himself, and thus the redemption will come.[91] Saadia mentions that nearing the time of the resurrection, "at the helm and head of them will stand the descendant of Joseph, by virtue of his being a righteous and well-tried servant of God, greatly rewarded by his Master."[92] In this manner, sounding very much like a *midrashic* narration of the real

---

[90] Saadia Gaon ben Yosef, 301.

[91] Ibid, 430-435. (Even though Christians interpret that Elijah the prophet described in Malachi 3:23-24 represents John the Baptist, Jews still do not recognize this.)

[92] Ibid, 309.

Jesus, son of Joseph the Nazareth carpenter, Saadia Gaon declared that He would be responsible for the final resurrection before His manifestation as Messiah son of David, who "will bring with him a retinue of people and go to Jerusalem. Then if it be in the hands of Armilus [the Antichrist], he [Messiah ben David] will kill him and take it from him."[93]

This *Talmudic* idea of a Messiah *ben* Joseph may originally be in reference to the patriarch Joseph, who suffered greatly at the hands of his brothers and was later exalted as king in Egypt, but the "coincidence" that Jesus' earthly father was called Joseph is quite powerful, since Jesus could have actually been known as "*Yeshua ben Yosef.*" And all Christians agree that the first coming of Jesus represents His priestly role of Messiah *ben* Joseph, whose righteous atoning death obtained our access to the Father, while His return will represent His kingly role as son of David.

b. Repentance necessary for redemption

According to other early writings (for example, B. Sanhedrin 97b, Y. Taanit 4:8, 68d, and Exod. Rabbah 25:12), the Jews need to repent before the Messiah can come. They state that when Israel repents and conforms to God's will, it will recover its Eden, and God's original plan will be realized at last. Their obedience should include performing good deeds or observing at least one Sabbath according to God's standards.[94]

Saadia Gaon also said that the future "Redemption" will come about through one of two possible occurrences: the first would be

---

[93] Ibid, 304.

[94] Jacob Neusner (ed. in chief), *Dictionary of Judaism in the Biblical Period: 450 BCE to 600 CE*, edited by William Scott Green (Peabody, Mass: Hendrickson, 1999), 204.

when all Israel repents at once, or the second, when God's timing becomes fulfilled. "Should our repentance…fall short, we would have to linger until the period of the end is fulfilled, some of us being subjected to punishment and others to trials."[95] Saadia Gaon clarified that if Israel does not repent, the events related to the *Messiah ben Yoseph* will have to come to pass. But if Israel repents, the previous events can be dispensed with, and the *Messiah ben David* will suddenly manifest himself. Nevertheless, Christians understand that the *Messiah ben Yosef* cannot be dispensed with, and both repentance and God's timing are the vital controlling elements in the fulfillment of this redemption event.

Neusner declares that redemption is promised to all Jews as a nation, except for the most recalcitrant of sinners. He adds that this repentance needs to be done on a personal level, because repentance and meticulous observance of the Law is necessary for Jews to "individually earn their personal portion in the coming world."[96]

c. **Human atonement for sin**

Early Biblical precepts specified that the sacrifice of an undefiled animal was the only means of atonement for purification of sin and defilement. After the destruction of the Temple, when animal sacrifice was no longer available, the Rabbis accepted repentance, fasting, prayer, and charity as a means of atonement. Personal suffering, exile, and death were also approved methods of atonement: *"May my death be an expiation for all my sins"* is a prayer recited when a Jew approaches his moment of death (*Sanhedrin Makkot* 6:2). Thus, Neusner claims that Israel can achieve atonement through its own death and

---

[95] Saadia Gaon Ben Yosef, 295.

[96] Ibid.

resurrection,[97] but this reflects the idea that the nation of Israel can be atoned for by itself.

On the other hand, the Jewish author Raphael Patai admits that there was an early belief where Isaiah 53 referred to a person who would suffer and die (the "servant"), providing atonement for all of Israel.[98] But he adds that most Jews nowadays interpret Isaiah 53 as referring to the nation of Israel, since they believe that, "psychologically, the Suffering Servant is but a projection and personification of Suffering Israel."

A little before the 1st century, there also appeared a *midrash* about how Isaac willingly bound himself up for the *Akedah*, and his "martyrdom" was perceived as an atonement for his people. The *midrash* states that Isaac's ashes were raised to life anew by the power of God.[99] The New Testament letter to the Hebrews refers to this tradition as a type of resurrection (Heb. 11:17-19). In this manner, Isaac's participation in the formalization of God's covenant with Abraham and Israel is parallel to Jesus' participation in permitting the Gentiles to enter into covenant with the same God of Abraham.[100]

Christians are clear that repentance and atonement produces personal salvation, which also leads to community redemption. Atonement of our sins can only produce forgiveness through the *"mediator of a new covenant"* (Heb. 9:15), namely Jesus the Messiah. Christians believe that He was the perfect and unblemished sacrifice whose atonement *"...redeems them from the transgressions committed under*

---

[97] Chilton and Neusner, *Classical Christianity and Rabbinic Judaism*, 237.

[98] Raphael Patai, *The Messiah Texts* (NY: Avon Books, 1979), xxxiii.

[99] Levenson, *The Death and Resurrection of the Beloved Son: The Transformation of Child Sacrifice in Judaism and Christianity* (New Haven: Yale University, 2006), 199.

[100] Ibid, 199.

the first covenant" (Heb. 9:15). His blood is more effective than that of goats or bulls in order to clean the conscience from dead works (v. 14).

d. Unity of many Gentiles and Jews prior to resurrection

Isaiah 56:8 says: *"Yet others I will gather to them, to those already gathered,"* clearly implying that many Gentiles will be joined to Israel at the time when He gathers His own people. It is remarkable that Saadia Gaon said that *"when those of the nations of the world…who are alive unite with the living among the Jewish believers,…the resurrection of the dead will take place…"*[101] Saadia Gaon here did not mean to imply that the "Jewish believers" are Jewish Christians, but rather honest God-fearing Jews. Even though Saadia denied that all Gentiles would participate in the resurrection, he stated that there would be a "unity" between some living Gentiles and the living Jews, which would then trigger the resurrection of the dead.

The New Testament confirms this spiritual unity prior to the resurrection from the dead, since Jesus also said: *"…I have other sheep that are not of this fold. I must bring them also, and they will listen to my voice. So there will be one flock, one shepherd"* (Jn. 10:16). The apostle Paul stated that Jesus reconciled both groups into one so that believing Gentiles can become *"fellow citizens with the saints"* (Eph. 2:19), implying that these saints are actually the righteous Jewish saints. Christians, who have received God's mercy, as well as Jews, are His *"chosen race, a royal priesthood, a holy nation, a people for his own possession"* (1 Pet. 2:9).

---

[101] Saadia Gaon Ben Yosef, 309.

e. Personal/National resurrection, Messianic Age, World to Come

Early Judaism before Jesus' time made many attempts to reconcile the conflicting elements of the end-time scenario, especially "the nationalistic, this-worldly eschatology with the universalistic, individualistic, other-worldly eschatology..."[102] The elements were so interwoven that they were difficult to view separately and place in some form of chronological order. This includes the timing of the resurrection. It was usually placed before the Messianic Kingdom on earth, also known as the "Days of the Messiah," which would then be followed by the Everlasting World or Age to Come. During the Days of the Messiah, each one would be recipient of divine guidance, as Jeremiah 31:34 states: *"...for they shall all know Me..."* They will all be able to recognize each other, starting from the leaders to all the common folk.

Early Christians also had this struggle, but generally agreed on the same timetable because the Old Testament served as basis to their common conceptions. But there was a general tendency to present the future as an eternal life *"with Christ"* (Rom. 8:17). Peter described it as *"an inheritance that is imperishable, undefiled, and unfading, kept in heaven for you, who by God's power are being guarded through faith for a salvation* **ready to be revealed in the last time**" (1 Pet. 1:4-5). This inheritance is "kept" in heaven but does not mean that this life will be in heaven. After a period of 1,000 years during the Messianic Kingdom on earth, both believe that there will be a new heaven and new earth, or Age to Come, of a very different reality.

---

[102] Sigmund Mowinckel, *He That Cometh: The Messiah Concept in the Old Testament and Later Judaism*, trans. G. W. Anderson (Grand Rapids: Eerdmans, 2005), 777.

10

Significance of Proposed Theory

What is very significant in this theory is the fact that both Christians and Jews expect a similar outcome from the resurrection of the righteous and after the final events have transpired. Just as Daniel 9:24 describes God's ultimate goal, which is *"to finish the transgression, to put an end to sin, and to atone for iniquity, to bring in everlasting righteousness, to seal both vision and prophet, and to anoint a most holy place,"* we can describe these more fully in the following manner:

a. Jewish/Christian Unity through Resurrection

Madigan and Levenson propose that, even though Martin Luther taught that Paul's central theological doctrine was righteousness by faith, Luther was merely looking at Paul from his 16th century lenses rather than from true 1st century lenses.[103] Paul's main theme was actually to experience a similar suffering and death as Christ did, and also the power of Christ's resurrection from the dead to a future life:

---

[103] Kevin J. Madigan and Jon D. Levenson, *Resurrection: The Power of God for Christians and Jews* (New Haven: Yale University Press, 2008), 35.

"I count all things to be loss…for whom I have suffered the loss of all things…so that I may gain Christ,…that I may know Him and the power of His resurrection and the fellowship of His sufferings…that I may attain to the resurrection from the dead" (Phil. 3:8-11).

Paul also saw baptism as a preview of the future resurrection. Christians can rest assured that God will ultimately raise their bodies from the dead because they are already united with Christ through baptism: *"For if we have become united with Him in the likeness of His death, certainly we shall also be in the likeness of His resurrection"* (Rom. 6:5).

Ellis states that Paul, as a Pharisee, already believed in the resurrection of the dead before becoming a follower of Jesus, and his encounter with the risen Christ did not initiate but rather confirmed his Pharisaic belief.[104] "It convinced him that Jesus was sent by the Father, that Jesus was the Messiah, and that with Jesus' resurrection there had begun the beginning of the end—the turning point of all history, the time when God would fulfill his messianic promises to Israel and the world."[105]

Paul also visualized the resurrection of the believers in a collective or communal manner. This is an event that will be experienced by all the congregation of God's people. *"For as in Adam all die, so also in Christ all will be made alive"* (1 Cor. 15:22). As Madigan and Levenson point out: "The resurrection of the community, not the individual, is primary. Paul thinks of the body of Christ as eternal, in much the same way that the vision of the dry bones in Ezekiel 37 thinks of

---

[104] Peter F. Ellis, *Seven Pauline letters* (Collegeville, MN: The Order of St. Benedict, 1982), 3, http://books.google.com/books?hl=en&lr=&id=VT3URW2QBs UC&oi=fnd&pg= PR9&ots= AiM75ZlFO0& sig=Bta6Sz9iefdJpvR3sK3VdgwPs 6Q#v=onepage&q=&f=false (accessed December 17, 2009).

[105] Ellis, 5.

Israel as eternal."[106] Thus, Paul did not cease to think in a collective manner after becoming a Christian, but transferred the same Jewish notion of God's people to the church and to a collective redemption in the latter days. And it wasn't that the church came to substitute Israel in God's plans, but that the Gentile church came to belong to the previous body of God's people through the New Covenant, and God's purposes would become totally fulfilled once all Israel was redeemed by its Messiah (Romans 11).

Above all, Paul emphasized that every believer needs to be changed, as referred to directly in 1 Corinthians 15:51: *"...we will not all sleep, but we will all be changed."* He referred to this as a *"mystery"* that would take place at the precise moment of the resurrection, *"in the twinkling of an eye, at the last trumpet..."* (v. 52). This must be experienced by all who are going to participate in God's Kingdom and live forever. Thus, at the sound of that trumpet, our body will undergo a physical transformation and become "re-created."

And since Paul was a Jew, he also held the understanding that the literal bones of the dead needed re-creating. "It was the bones, therefore, that were the primary subject of the resurrection."[107] In this hope, Jews at that time allowed the body to decompose, and then they collected the bones and placed them in ossuaries. If a body were totally destroyed by either mutilation or burning, they believed that God could still re-create the body out of nothing (*ex nihilo*). Another way of visualizing this process is by means of becoming *"clothed"* with our *"heavenly dwelling"* (2 Cor. 5:2). In order that the perishable and mortal become imperishable and immortal, we must *"put on,"* or *"becomes clothed with,"* a new reality.

---

[106] Madigan and Levenson, *Resurrection: The Power of God for Christians and Jews*, 35.

[107] Bruce D. Chilton and Jacob Neusner, *Classical Christianity and Rabbinic Judaism: Comparing Theologies* (Grand Rapids: Baker Academic, 2004), 61.

There are many references in the Old Testament Scriptures that illustrate Israel's resurrection once they have been saved/redeemed. A wonderful prophetic picture is found in Exodus 6:1-13, the story of Israel's redemption from Egypt during the Passover, which can be seen to represent a future fulfillment.

> *"I am the LORD, and I will bring you out from under the burdens of the Egyptians, and I will deliver you from slavery to them, and I will redeem you with an outstretched arm and with great acts of judgment. I will take you to be my people, and I will be your God..."* (Ex. 6:6-7).

This promise contains elements very similar to a resurrection and possession of the Messianic kingdom: *"I will bring you out..., I will deliver you from..., I will redeem you with..., I will take you to be my people..., I will bring you into..."* Thus, in the same manner that God took His people out of their slavery into the Promised Land, He will also take them out of their present spiritual slavery into the Promised Kingdom.

We must notice that the Jewish people will be taken out from their present place and then brought into another place. This is the final goal of God's eternal Covenant with His people, this transformation between one present condition into a different future condition, as is confirmed in Exodus 3:8, when God will come down (in the form of their Messiah) and take them up (or gather them) out of the land: *"I have come down to deliver them out of the hand of the Egyptians and to bring them up out of that land..."*

b. Final Spiritual/Cosmic Fulfillment of God's Purposes

Regarding what the resurrection will ultimately accomplish, both Christians and Jews agree that the resurrection of the dead will fulfill all their dreams and hopes on the cosmic level, similar to Daniel 9:24. According to Levenson, resurrection was the key element in a "whole panorama of redemptive and re-creative events that characterize the rabbinic vision of the end of history." This includes "the liberation of the Jews from subjugation to Gentile rule, the ingathering of the exile to the Land of Israel, the enthronement of the God of Israel, the reconstruction of Jerusalem as God's dwelling, and the coming of the messianic king."[108] The Jewish orthodox *Artscroll Prayerbook* expresses its hope and faith in this manner:

> "The dead will live again in the Messianic era, when the world will attain a new spiritual and physical level of perfection. Those who have not been found too unworthy to enter this exalted state will live again to enjoy it."[109]

The Christian statement of faith is very similar:

> *"This is evidence of the righteous judgment of God, that you may be considered worthy of the kingdom of God... when the Lord Jesus is revealed from heaven with his mighty angels in flaming fire... when he comes on that day to be glorified in his saints..."* (2 Thess. 1:5-10).

---

[108] Levenson, *Resurrection and the Restoration of Israel*, 5-7.

[109] *The Complete Artscroll Siddur, Weekly, Sabbath, Festival*,12-13.

Ultimately, the resurrection event will transform the world as we know it, and will initiate a new, beautiful, and unimaginable reality, far too great for words. It will produce the following results in the spiritual/cosmic order:

1) Tension between God's mercy and justice resolved

Eschatology is also all about what happens at the end of each persons' life, depending on their present earthly life. Now is the time to define our personal future. God's justice requires that He repay to each whatever they have sown, whether eternal life with God or eternal condemnation without God. But in God's mercy, He has given us the opportunity to live according to His will. *"I call heaven and earth to witness against you today, that I have set before you life and death, blessing and curse. Therefore choose life, that you and your offspring may live"* (Deut. 30:19). *"For God so loved the world, that he gave his only Son, that whoever believes in him should not perish but have eternal life"* (Jn. 3:16).

Chilton and Neusner, in their co-authored book entitled *Classical Christianity and Rabbinic Judaism: Comparing Theologies,* also point out that the doctrine of God's omnipotence precipitates an apparent conflict between His justice and His mercy. "This conflict is resolved only with the doctrine of the resurrection of the dead: the judgment and the victory over the grave..."[110]

From the Jewish perspective, "without judgment and eternal life for the righteous, this world's imbalance cannot be righted, nor can God's justice be revealed."[111] But through God's mercy to those who are deemed worthy of a "portion in the world to come," He will grant them a return to Eden and eternal life.

---

[110] Chilton and Neusner, *Classical Christianity and Rabbinic Judaism*, 223.
[111] Ibid, 12-13.

Regarding this tension in Christian terms, Jesus' resurrection and victory over the grave has resolved the seemingly contradictory divine characteristics of justice and mercy, and people can be found to be worthy to inherit the Kingdom of God.

2) Human immortality obtained in imperishable bodies

According to Neusner, the majority of Jewish people imagine human immortality in the context of a bodily resurrection. Though man's body was not created to be immortal in this lifetime, his immortal soul received a body from God, and "at the time of the body's death, [the soul] is taken back to God, where it awaits the time of the resurrection and the world to come. Then it will be restored to that same body,"[112] yet in imperishable form.

This is similar to mainline Christianity in that this resurrection of the dead represents a return of the soul to its previous physical body, but of an imperishable kind. *"For this perishable body must put on the imperishable, and this mortal body must put on immortality"* (1 Cor. 15:53).

3) Humanity restored to the Divine image

Both Jews and Christians believe that the first Adam and Eve ruined the divine image that God had placed in them at creation, and God's master plan of restoring humanity to His own image and likeness is part of both eschatologies. Neusner declares: "This [restoration] is a hope Christianity also shares with Judaism."[113]

Christianity also has the vision of becoming *"partakers of the divine nature"* in the Messiah (2 Pet. 1:4). And *"just as we have borne the image*

---

[112] Neusner (ed. in chief), *Dictionary of Judaism in the Biblical Period*, 311.

[113] Chilton and Neusner, *Classical Christianity and Rabbinic Judaism*, 255.

of the man of dust, we shall also bear the image of the man of heaven" (1 Cor. 15:49).

4) God's promises fulfilled to all His people

Both Christianity and Judaism have usually portrayed death as an opportunity, not a misfortune. "Resurrection, as usually defined, promises actual life to individual persons within God's global transformation of all things."[114] This reversal of death, for Christianity as well as for Judaism, is an example of the incomparable power of God and His trustworthy faithfulness, a God who fulfills His promises to all His people.

The discourse on faith in Hebrews chapter 11 speaks about certain "heroes" of the Jewish faith achieving the reward of their faith and promised inheritance. This promised reward and inheritance is the resurrection of the dead and their participation in the Kingdom of God. The chapter concludes with:

> *"And all these, though commended through their faith, did not receive what was promised, since God had provided something better for us, that apart from us they should not be made perfect"* (Heb. 11:39-40).

The author of Hebrews points out that the Jewish people of faith cannot be made perfect, or raised, apart from the new Gentile believers in Christ, who have also been included in the covenant by means of the same faith in God and His Messiah.

---

[114] Ibid.

11

How Should we Respond?

Seeing these common perspectives between Jews and Christians, authors Juster and Intrater believe that "God has worked it out so that if we are to walk in the fullness of His plan for us, the Gentiles will have to receive from the Jews in certain areas, and the Jews will have to receive from the Gentiles in other areas."[115] This is definitely a must, in order for God to accomplish all that He desires in and for His people, according to Daniel 9:24.

a. Our Christian Responsibility

Most Christians believe that God's promises will eventually be fulfilled, though the timing is not totally clear. In any case, there is something that we should be working on as we look forward in trust and hope. Traditional Christians must learn to be more tolerant of the Jewish faith and traditions, realizing that Jews are expressing their faith in God in an honest manner as Christians express their own faith in God. Jews have been worshipping the true God far longer than the Christians, so there is much that we can learn from

---

[115] Juster and Intrater, 146.

them. Even though Christians do not need to keep all the Jewish traditions and celebrations, we can respectfully participate in the feasts as they apply to the Messiah. But this does not give us the right to appropriate Judaism for ourselves as the "true Israel," since we are just the new kids on the block. On the other hand, those who already understand this can help other Christians to change their negative perception of Jews, and thus perhaps prepare the way for their acceptance of the Messiah.

Christians should also become more accepting of the "different" flavor and emphasis of "Messianic believers" (Jewish believers in *Yeshua*). There is nothing wrong with their desire to blend their Jewish background with essential Christian doctrines, so long as it is done within a proper Biblical balance. The New Testament Scriptures should be their guide in this regard. Moreover, many Gentile believers are becoming attracted and identified with this new expression of Messianic faith. Some may even believe that this type of "Messianism" is more Biblical than the ecclesiastical structure that was developed from the 4th century onward. In this new style, Christians can become more "completed" by accepting their Jewish origins, just as Jewish people become more "completed" when they accept *Yeshua* as their true Messiah.

There is something else that Christians can do in the meantime, which is to spread this news about the Jewish Messiah to the nations. Jesus said: *"And this gospel of the kingdom will be proclaimed throughout the whole world as a testimony to all nations, and then the end will come"* (Matt. 24:14). This Gospel message should include the Jewish heritage of our faith and our ongoing relationship with the People of the Covenant, since without it our Gospel would lack its foundation. That is also part of our history, and it only makes sense when we include the whole story. Our origins lie in Biblical Judaism, and we will ultimately share a future together.

On the other hand, missionary efforts to the Jews can be very controversial and even counterproductive at times, since they do not usually take into account that the Jewish people are already a God-fearing nation based on a holy covenant. They may lack the fulfillment of God's covenant in their lives through the Messiah, but Christians can still respect them as God's people. The best way for Christians to share their faith with Jews is by living out a life wholly according to God's intent, healing past hurts caused by centuries of Christian persecution and Anti-Semitism, and helping Jews to change their negative perception of Christians through their honest love and respect. Showing a Spirit-filled life is what Christians are called to do among the Jewish people, thus provoking them to jealousy (Rom. 11:11). The rest is up to God. After all, Jesus said: *"No one can come to me unless the Father who sent me draws him…"* (Jn. 6:44).

And finally, Christians should be praying with joy and hope for our ultimate unity with the Jewish people to become a reality, because that is what God Himself desires: *"…Rejoice, O Gentiles, with his people"* (Rom. 15:10). He wants to prove His faithfulness to His covenants and promises of old.

> *"So when God desired to show more convincingly to the heirs of the promise* [the descendants of Abraham] *the unchangeable character of His purpose, He guaranteed it with an oath, so that by two unchangeable things* [**His promise and His purpose**], *in which it is impossible for God to lie, we…might have strong encouragement to hold fast to the hope set before us. We have this as a sure and steadfast anchor of the soul…"* (Heb. 6:17-19).

Thus, we are to live out our days with this longing, but also with patience, as though that day will soon arrive. *"Be patient, therefore, brothers, until the coming of the Lord…Establish your hearts, for the coming of the Lord is at hand"* (James 5:7-8).

b. An Imagined Frontier

Thus, since both Jews and Christians believe in a final resurrection with common elements and similar results, each can be fellow believers in the same Messiah even though we may see Him from our own perspective as He fulfills both of our expectations.

In spite of these similarities, Neusner still seeks to "sharpen the lines of difference" because he believes that this would open "a new path of religious dialogue."[116] But in contrast, instead of seeing Christianity and Judaism as a "parting of the ways," the Jewish academic Daniel Boyarin rightly defines them as belonging to the same territory with an imagined frontier, where an artificial borderline has been imposed.[117] Thus, the blurred distinctions between Christians and Jews are actually mainly imaginary borderlines.

Skarsaune agrees that early Christianity and Rabbinic Judaism were merely virtual "ideological constructions," and not much more.[118] In fact, early "Jewish Christians" became a category almost impossible to distinguish within the broader Jewish-Christian

[116] Jacob Neusner, *A Rabbi Talks with Jesus* (Montreal: McGill-Queen's Univ. Press, 2001), 12.

[117] Daniel Boyarin, *Border Lines: The Partition of Judaeo-Christianity* (Philadelphia: Univ. of Pennsylvania Press, 2004), 5.

[118] Oskar Skarsaune, "Fragments of Jewish Christian Literature Quoted in Some Greek and Latin Fathers" in *Jewish Believers in Jesus: The Early Centuries*, edited by Oskar Skarsaune and Reidar Hvalvik (Peabody, Mass: Hendrickson Publ., 2007), 747.

continuum. He also agrees with Boyarin's position in that early historians and religious leaders began to redefine their respective faiths and practices as intrinsically incompatible with each other just so as to defend their own positions. Though it is possible to admit that this spiritual continuum was smoother before the Emperor Constantine and the creation of a Christian establishment, it is still important to visualize any real borderline in modern times as merely imaginary so as to correct any model that may separate Jews and Christians.[119]

All in all, Christians should understand more about Jewish eschatology, and Jews should understand more about Christian eschatology. We are much more similar to each other than most usually want to admit. We must focus on promoting a mature mutual understanding and respect between Christians and Jews, agreeing on what is common to both, and then allow God to take care the rest. True, the huge divides that exist inside each of the faiths need resolving, but maybe the study of eschatology can help both groups to take their corresponding step. If we both share the same pieces of the eschatological puzzle, how we can help but end up with the same picture? But it is important to state that we all must enter into an intimate relationship with God and His Messiah through the New Covenant. Once this personal spiritual condition is settled by the indwelling of God's Spirit in the believer, it does not matter what we call ourselves. This is the only guarantee for our participation in the resurrection and the World to Come, no matter whether we are Jew or Gentile.

Finally, Levenson points out that, rather than distinguishing Judaism as the mother faith and Christianity as the daughter faith, "it would be more accurate to say that Rabbinic Judaism and Christianity

---

[119] Skarsaune, 748-750.

are...siblings, sister religions whose parent was Second Temple Judaism and whose more distant ancestors were still earlier phases of the religion of Israel."[120] Moreover, Daniel Boyarin believes that "they are twins, joined at the hip."[121] Both Judaism and Christianity took some routes that seem to be very distant from their own roots, but in general, both faiths share the basic conviction that "the God of justice [will] soon intervene to bring an end to the present age and inaugurate the Age to Come."[122]

---

[120] Madigan and Levenson, *Resurrection*, 235.

[121] Boyarin, 5.

[122] Madigan and Levenson, *Resurrection*, 7.

Appendices

APPENDIX 1:

Below is a table highlighting past empires and events described in Daniel, other present-day governments hinted at in the text, plus things that could still lie in our future, including the strengthening of the Antichrist, the resurrection of the saints, the Antichrist's dominion, and the Messianic Kingdom.

DANIEL'S HISTORIC AND END-TIME GOVERNMENTS

KINGDOMS	Chap. 2	Chap. 7	Chap. 8	Chap. 9	Chap. 11	Chap. 12
1. Babylonian Empire	Statue's head: Gold [Nebuchad-nezzar] (Dan. 2:38)	Lion with eagle wings – also man (Dan. 7:4)		1st Temple destroyed (Dan. 9:11-12)		
2. Median/ Persian Empire	Statue's chest/ arms: silver [Cyrus] (Dan. 2:39)	Bear with 2 sides (Dan. 7:5)	Ram and 2 horns: 2nd higher than the first (Dan. 8:3, 20)	Temple & Jerusalem restored in troubled times (Dan. 9:25).		
3. Greek Empire	Statue's waist/thigh are bronze [Alexander the Great] (Dan. 2:39)	Leopard with 4 wings and 4 heads (Dan. 7:6)	Male goat with 1 horn tramples ram - horn broken and 4 new come up (Dan.8:4-21)			

4. Roman Empire ["Great Tribulation" begins for Israel, including the death of the Prince of the Covenant, the destruction of the 2nd Temple, and Israel's dispersion]	Statue's legs: iron [various Roman emperors] (Dan. 2:40)	It will be terrifying and strong, different from all previous kingdoms. It will devour the whole earth, and trample it down, and break it to pieces (Dan. 7:7).	One out of the 4 horns grows strong, and reaches the glorious land. It throws down the **Prince of Hosts.** Removes the regular sacrifices (Dan. 8:9-11).	**"Anointed One"** comes but is cut off. God makes a Covenant with "the many" and puts end to sacrifices. People of a later "prince" destroys the [Second] Temple and Jerusalem (Dan. 9:26-27).	He destroys the glorious land. Armies will be swept away, even the **Prince of the Covenant.** He profanes the temple and takes away the regular burnt offering (Dan. 11:21-22, 31a).	The regular burnt offering is taken away (Dan. 12:11).

5. Times of the Gentiles [Islam is birthed and spreads, Temple Mount in Jerusalem is trampled by the Gentiles]	Wears out the saints and they will be given into his hand for a time, times, and half a time (Dan. 7:25).		"One who makes desolate" will put an abomination on a wing [of the Temple Mount] (Dan. 9:27)	Sets up the abomination that causes desolation with the help of a foreign god. (Dan. 11:3b, 36-39).	Abomination that makes desolation is set up (Dan. 12:11).
6. Extension of time [Muslim Ottoman Empire destroys Christian Byzantine Empire]	"Other little horn" will arise from the fourth beast. He will fall, yet will return after a season and a time (Dan. 7:8, 12)	Desolation of the sanctuary for 2,300 evenings and mornings (Dan. 8:14)	Desolations will come as a flood for one week (Dan. 9:26)	The wise will understand, though for some days they will be persecuted (Dan. 11:33)	Many will purify themselves but the wicked will act more wickedly (Dan. 12:10)

7. **"Tribulation of those days"** [Beginnings of the renewed Muslim Empire, though Antichrist not yet fully revealed.]		Continued desolations while the sanctuary continues to be trampled on (Dan. 8:13-14)	Desolations continue (Dan. 9:26)	Many will be refined, purified, and made white, until the time of the end (Dan. 11:35)	Times of trouble for God's holy people continue until their power is shattered (Dan. 12:1, 7)
8. **Resurrection of the saints**					Saints will rise to everlasting life (12:2)

9. Antichrist's global Caliphate	Statue's feet: partly of iron + partly clay ["Chrislam"] (Dan. 2:41-43)	"Another" related beast will also speak great things against God, and will think he is greater than his companions (Dan. 7:20).		He will pitch his palace in Jerusalem. He will honor those who acknow-ledge him, make them rulers over many, and divide the land for a price (Dan. 11:40-45)

10. God's Wrath [Judgment against the Antichrist government]	God will bring to an end all kingdoms, which are broken by the "Stone" (Dan. 2:44-45)	His dominion shall be taken away, consumed and destroyed to the end (Dan. 7:26)	He will be broken, but not by human hand (Dan. 8:25)	Decreed end is poured out on the "desolator." (Dan. 9:27)	He will ultimately come to his end (Dan. 11:45)	Others rise to eternal contempt (Dan. 12:2)
11. Messianic Kingdom	God establishes His great mountain forever (Dan. 2:35, 44)	Messianic kingdom will be given to God's saints forever (Dan. 7:18, 27)	Sanctuary is restored to its rightful state (Dan. 8:14)	- transgressions finish - sin ends - iniquity is atoned for - righteousness enters - vision is sealed - Most Holy is anointed (Dan. 9:24)	It all still awaits the appointed time (Dan. 11:35).	Those whose names are in the Book of Life will shine bright like the sky forever (Dan. 12:1-3)

APPENDIX 2:

Below is a table that compares the different types of tribulation with world powers as described in Matthew 24, Daniel 7 and 11, Revelation 13, and 2 Thessalonians 2. All four sources give different details, but they all share several elements in common. There are some events that pertain to the past and present extended period of tribulations, plus the coming "tribulation of those days" that still lies in our future. This will culminate with the signs that need to occur right before Jesus appears to gather His people.

Tribulation Period	World Powers	Matthew 24	Daniel 7 & 11	Revelation 13	2 Thess. 2
Past "Great Tribulation" to **present** "normal" tribulations	Roman and Muslim Ottoman Empire	Destruction of Jerusalem, wars, famines, persecutions, etc. (24:5-15)	"Other Little" Horn (7:8, 20-21) (11:31b-39)	First Beast from the Sea (13:1-10)	Mystery of Lawlessness (2:7)
Future "tribulation of those days" and final "signs"	Greater influence of Islam and universalism	Lawlessness increases and love of many grows cold (24:12)	Wise are refined (11:35)	Saints endure (13:10)	Wicked refuse the truth (2:10)
		RESURRECTION	OF GOD'S	SAINTS	
Antichrist's Global Subjugation (does not qualify as "tribulation")	United Muslim Caliphate (+ UN, EU, & Vatican)	Tribes of the earth will mourn (24:30)	"Different" Horn (7:24-25) (11:40-45)	Second Beast from the Earth (13:11-18)	Man of Lawlessness revealed (2:3-4)

APPENDIX 3:

This table shows the significance of the various Seals of Revelation, comparing them to the Gospels and to Daniel 9 and 12.

Historic Time	Seven Seals of Revelation	Olivet Discourse	Daniel 9 & 12
"Great Tribulation"		Jerusalem will be destroyed, and the abomination of desolations will be set up in the Holy place.	The Temple will be destroyed and the abomination that makes desolation will be set up.
Normal tribulations for 20 centuries	1. First Seal = wars and conquests	Wars and rumors of war; nation will rise against nation.	There will be a time of trouble as never before.
Normal tribulations for 20 centuries	2. Second Seal = tyrants and assassinations	Lawlessness, assassinations	To the end there shall be wars and desolations.
Normal tribulations for 20 centuries	3. Third Seal = financial disasters and famines	Famines, earthquakes	
Normal tribulations for 20 centuries	4. Fourth Seal = death and pestilences	Pestilences, terrorism	
Normal tribulations for 20 centuries	5. Fifth Seal = Martyrdom of God's people	Persecution, martyrdom, and dispersion	The power of God's people will be shattered.

Present days before the "tribulation of those days"		False prophets will lead Christians astray and the love of people will grow cold. The Gospel will be proclaimed throughout the world.	Many will run to and fro, and knowledge will greatly increase. The wise will purify themselves and will understand.
"Tribulation of those days"	6. Sixth Seal and Six Trumpets = Signs in heaven and on earth, islands and mountains disappear, upheavals in nature, wars, and destruction of a third of all things.	There will be terrors and great signs from heaven. Sun and moon will be darkened, stars will fall, powers of heaven will shake, seas will roar.	The wicked will not understand, and will continue to act wickedly.
After the heavenly signs	7. "… *a loud voice from heaven saying to them* [**His witnesses**], *'Come up here!' And they went up to heaven in a cloud…*" (Rev. 11:12).	*"And then he will send out the angels and gather **his elect** from the four winds…"* (Mk. 13:27).	*"But at that time **your people** shall be delivered, everyone whose name shall be found written in the book"* (Dan. 12:1).

APPENDIX 4:

The table below gives a quick summary of each Trumpet and its possible effects, which could symbolize events that will occur at different moments in time and in different locations, rather than literally, simultaneously, or consecutively.

Trumpet	Symbolic Action	Possible Real Effect
1	hail and fire fall to earth and cause fires	Widespread contamination of land, trees, and vegetation
2	something like a mountain falls into the sea	Widespread contamination of oceans, death of sea creatures and tidal waves
3	a great star falls on the rivers	Widespread contamination of rivers and sources of drinking water
4	sun, moon, and stars darken	Widespread contamination of air so thick that sun, moon, and stars are barely visible
5	the bottomless pit is opened and an army of demons torment those **who do not have God's seal** for *"5 months"*	Satan and his demons provoke widespread suffering using newly developed weapons of warfare, such as tanks, helicopters, and airplanes (World War 2?)
6	four angels of the Euphrates are released	Widespread war revolving around the Middle East with enormous armies, more advanced weapons of warfare, including digital and nuclear weapons
7	a loud voice from heaven calls: "Come up!"	God's people are raised

APPENDIX 5:

Below is a table that shows the Bible text where all the Lord's Feasts are described, and then how they are fulfilled by Jesus, the son of God and Messiah:

Feast	Bible Text	Fulfillment in Jesus
Sabbath	Lev. 23:3	He is our eternal rest
Passover	Lev. 23:5	He is our Passover Lamb
Unleavened Bread	Lev. 23:6-8	He is the sinless Bread of Life
First Fruits	Lev. 23:9-14	He rose as Firstfruits from the dead
Weeks	Lev. 23:15-22	He sent us His Holy Spirit
Trumpets	**Lev. 23:23-25**	**He calls His people to repentance**
Day of Atonement	Lev. 23:26-32	Israel will be forgiven, and then saved/redeemed through the resurrection
Tabernacles	Lev. 23:33-36, 39-43	He will return with His people to establish His millennial kingdom

Bibliography

_____. *The Holy Bible*. C. I. Scofield, ed. NY: Oxford University Press, 1945.

_____. *The Holy Bible, English Standard Version*. Wheaton, Illinois: Crossway Bibles, 2007.

Archer, Gleason L. (ed.) and others. *Three Views on the Rapture: Pre-, Mid-, or Post-Tribulation*. Stanley N. Gundry, series editor. Grand Rapids, MI: Zondervan: 1996.

Arnold III, William. *The Post-Tribulation Rapture*. Kindle, 1999.

Augustine. *Treatise against the Jews*, Chap. 10, posted by Roger Pearse. https://www.roger- pearse.com/weblog/2015/06/11/augustines-treatise-against -the-jews/comment-page-1/ (accessed August 19, 2018).

Barclay, William. "The Letters to Philippians, Colossians and Thessalonians" in *The Daily Study Bible*. Glasgow, Scotland: The Saint Andrew Press, 1961.

Barker, Kenneth L and John R. Kohlenberger III. *The Expositor's Bible Commentary*, Abridged Ed. Grand Rapids, MI: Zondervan, 1994.

Ben Yosef, Saadia Gaon. "Concerning the Resurrection of the Dead in this World" in *The Book of Beliefs and Opinions,* Treatise VII. Translated by Samuel Rosenblatt. Massachusetts: Yale Press, 1948.

Bergman, Judith, *UN Launches All-out War on Free Speech*, https://www. gatestoneinstitute.org/14516/united-nations-free-speech (accessed July 10, 2019).

Biederwolf, William E. *The Second Coming Bible.* Grand Rapids, MI: Baker Books, 1972.

Bloomfield, Arthur E. *Before the Last Battle Armageddon.* Minneapolis, MN: Bethany Fellowship, 1971.

_____. *Signs of His Coming: A Study of the Olivet Discourse.* Minneapolis, MN: Bethany Fellowship, 1962.

Boers, Hendrikus. "The Meaning of Christ's Resurrection in Paul" in *Resurrection: The Origin and Future of a Biblical Doctrine*, Faith and Scholarship Colloquies. New York: T & T Clark, 2006.

Boyarin, Daniel. *Border Lines: The Partition of Judaeo-Christianity.* Philadelphia: Univ. of Pennsylvania Press, 2004.

Brickner, David. *Future Hope: A Jewish Christian Look at the End of the World.* San Francisco, CA: Purple Pomegranate Productions, 1999.

Brown, Francis, S. R. Driver and Charles Briggs. *The Brown-Driver-Briggs Hebrew and English Lexicon.* Peabody, Mass: Hendrickson, 2001.

Brown, Raymond E. *An Introduction to the New Testament.* NY: Doubleday, 1997.

Bruce, F. F. "1 and 2 Thessalonians" in *Word Biblical Commentary*, Vol. 45. Mexico City, Mexico: Thomas Nelson, 1982.

Chafer, Lewis Sperry (Span. trans. by José María Chicol, M. Francisco Lievano, and Rodolfo Mendieta). *Teología Sistemática*, Tomo II, vol. IV, V, and VI. Milwaukee, WI: Publicaciones Españolas, Inc., 1986.

Chilton, Bruce D. Chilton and Jacob Neusner, *Classical Christianity and Rabbinic Judaism: Comparing Theologies*. Grand Rapids: Baker Academic, 2004.

Clarion Project, *How to Make Sense of US Withdrawal from Syria*, https://clarion project.org/how-to-make-sense-of-u-s-withdrawal-from-syria/ (accessed December 20, 2018).

Clouse, Robert G., Ed. *The Meaning of the Millennium: Four Views*, Downers Grove, Illinois: IVP Academic, 1977.

_____. "Rapture of the Church" in *Evangelical Dictionary of Theology*, 2nd ed. Grand Rapids, MI: Baker Academic, 2007.

Cohen, Abraham, *Everyman's Talmud*. New York: Schocken Books, 1995.

Currie, David B. *Rapture: The End-Times Error that Leaves the Bible Behind*. Manchester, NH: Sophia Institute Press, 2003.

Daley, Brian E. *The Hope of the Early Church: A Handbook of Patristic Eschatology*. Grand Rapids, MI: Baker Academic, 1991.

De Witt, Hans. "El Libro de Daniel: Persecución y Resistencia (Span.)" in *Revista de Interpretación Bíblica Latinoamericana - Los Libros Proféticos*, No. 35-36, Quito, Ecuador, 2000.

Didache, Early Christian Writings, chap. 16, trans. Roberts-Donaldson, http://www.earlychristianwritings.com/text/didache-roberts.html (accessed August 21, 2018).

Didache, four different translations in *Early Christian Writings*, chap. 16, http://www. earlychristianwritings.com/didache.html (accessed August 21, 2018).

Didache, interlinear Greek-English version by Facsimiliter, http:// facsimiliter.com/ Documents/DidacheIlnr.htm (accessed August 21, 2018).

Didache, interlinear Greek-English version by Psalm 119 Foundation, https://www. psalm11918.org /References/Apocrypha/The-Interlinear-Didache.html (accessed August 21, 2018).

Dunn, James D. G. *The Theology of Paul the Apostle.* Grand Rapids, MI: Eerdmans, 1998.

Eastman, Mark and Chuck Smith. *The Search for Messiah.* Costa Mesa, CA: The Word for Today and Joy Publ., 1996.

Ellis, Peter F. *Seven Pauline letters.* Collegeville, MN: The Order of St. Benedict, 1982. http://books.google.com/books?hl=en&lr=&id =VT3URW2QBsUC &oi=fnd&pg=PR9&ots=AiM75ZlFO0&sig =Bta6Sz9iefdJpvR3sK3VdgwPs6Q#v=onepage&q=&f=false (accessed December 17, 2009).

Elwell, Walter A. *Evangelical Dictionary of Theology*, 2nd ed. Grand Rapids, MI: Baker Academic, 2007.

Epistle of Barnabas, trans. Jackson H. Snyder and Theodore Dornan, adapted from Hoole's 1885 translation, http://www.jacksonsnyder.com/__yah/ manuscript-library/Bar-Nabba-final-021310.pdf (accessed August 28, 2018).

Erickson, Millard J. *Christian Theology*, 2nd ed. Grand Rapids, MI: Baker Academic, 1998.

_____. *A Basic Guide to Eschatology: Making Sense of the Millennium*. Grand Rapids, MI, Baker Books, 1998.

Eusebius. *Demostratio Evangelica*, Trans. W. J. Ferrar, IntraText Edition, Society for Promoting Christian Knowledge. London: The Macmillan Company, 1920. http://www.intratext.com/IXT/ENG0882/_P38.HTM (accessed September 20, 2018).

_____. *Ecclesiastical History*, Trans. Christian Frederick Crusé, Internet Archive. New York: Thomas N. Stanford, 1856. https://archive.org/details/ ecclesiasticalhi00euse/page/n8 (accessed August 17, 2018).

Fee, Gordon D. "The First and Second Letters to the Thessalonians" in *The New International Commentary on the New Testament*. Grand Rapids, MI: Eerdmans, 2009.

Ferguson, Everett. *Backgrounds of Early Christianity*. 3d ed. Grand Rapids, MI: Eerdmans, 2003.

Gatestone Institute, *Turkey Turns on America*, https://www. gatestoneinstitute. org/13470/turkey-turns-on-america (accessed December 24, 2018).

Gatestone Institute, *Next for Turkey? Nuclear Weapons!*, https://www. gatestone institute.org/14896/ turkey-erdogan-nuclear-weapons (accessed September 18, 2019).

Gerhard Kittel and Gerhard Friedrich, eds. *Theological Dictionary of the New Testament*, Vol. VIII, Geoffrey W. Bromiley, trans. Grand Rapids, MI: Eerdmans, 1968.

González, Justo L. *Historia del Cristianismo, Tomo 1.* Miami, FL: Unilit, 1994.

Grau, José. "Escatología Final de los Tiempos, Tomo VII" in *Curso de Formación Teológica Evangélica*. Barcelona, Spain: Editorial Clie, 1977.

Green, Gene L. "The Letters to the Thessalonians" in *The Pillar New Testament Commentary*. Grand Rapids, MI: Eerdmans, 2002.

Green, Jay P. *The Interlinear Bible, Hebrew-Greek-English*, 2nd ed. Peabody, Mass: Hendrickson, 1986.

Gruber, Daniel. *The Church and the Jews – the Biblical Relationship.* Springfield, MO: General Council of Assemblies of God Intercultural Ministries, 1991.

Grudem, Wayne. *Systematic Theology*. Grand Rapids, MI: Zondervan, 1994.

Gundry, Robert H. *The Church and the Tribulation: A Biblical Examination of Post-tribulationism*, Grand Rapids, MI: Zondervan Academie Books, 1973.

Guthrie, Donald. *New Testament Theology*. Downers Grove, IL: 1981.

Hedding, Malcolm. *Days of Destiny*. Durban, South Africa: Mallies Books, nd.

Humason, Brent D. *Rapture Fusion: Merging the Pre-Tribulation, Mid-Tribulation, Pre-Wrath, and Post-Tribulation Rapture Views into Something Better*. Columbia, SC: Self-published, 2018.

Ironside, H. A. *Lectures on Daniel the Prophet*. Neptune, NJ: Loiseaux Brothers, 1920.

Jamieson, Fausset and Brown. *One Volume Commentary*, Grand Rapids, MI: Associated Publishers and Authors, Inc., original 1871, republished n.d.

Jerusalem Center for Public Affairs, *Turkey's Expansionist Policy Exposed*, http://jcpa.org/turkeys-expansionist-policy-exposed/ (accessed January 30, 2019).

Juster, Dan and Asher (Keith) Intrater. *Israel, the Church, and the Last Days*. Shippensburg, PA: Destiny Image, 2003.

Lacunza, Manuel. *The Coming of Messiah in Glory and Majesty*, Vol. 1. Translated by Edward Irving. Fleet Street, London: Seeley and Son, 1827.

_____. *The Coming of Messiah in Glory and Majesty*, Vol. 2. Translated by Edward Irving. Fleet Street, London: Seeley and Son, 1827.

Ladd, George Eldon. *The Blessed Hope*. Grand Rapids, MI: Eerdmans, 1956.

_____. *A Commentary on the Revelation of John*. Grand Rapids, MI: Eerdmans, 1972.

LaHaye, Tim. *Revelation: Illustrated and Made Plain*. Grand Rapids: Zondervan, 1973.

Lalonde, Peter. *One World under Antichrist*. Eugene, Oregon: Harvest House Publishers, 1991.

Levenson, Jon D. *Resurrection and the Restoration of Israel: The Ultimate Victory of the God of Life*. New Haven: Yale University, 2006.

_____. *The Death and Resurrection of the Beloved Son: The Transformation of Child Sacrifice in Judaism and Christianity*. New Haven: Yale University, 1993.

Lewis, David Allen. *Prophecy 2000*. Green Forrest, AZ: New Leaf Press, 1992.

Lindsey, Hal. *The Late Great Planet Earth*. Grand Rapids, MI: Zondervan, 1970.

Lockyer, Herbert. *All the Messianic Prophecies of the Bible*, Grand Rapids, MI: Zondervan, 1973.

Madigan, Kevin J. and Jon D. Levenson. *Resurrection: The Power of God for Christians and Jews*. New Haven: Yale University Press, 2008.

Mare, W. Harold. "1 Corinthians." Pages 173-291 in *Romans - Galatians*. Vol. 10 of *The Expositor's Bible Commentary*. Grand Rapids: Zondervan, 1976.

McKeever, Jim. *Christians Will Go Through the Tribulation: And How to Prepare for It*. Medford, Oregon: Omega Publications, 1978.

_____. *Now You can Understand the Book of Revelation*. Medford, Oregon: Omega Publications, 1980.

Merrill, Eugene H. *Everlasting Dominion: A Theology of the Old Testament*. Nashville, TN: B & H, 2006.

Mitchell, Bob. *The Post Tribulation Rapture of the Church*. Columbia, SC: Self-published, 2018.

Moo, Douglas J. "The Case for Posttribulation Rapture position" in *Three Views on the Rapture: Pre-, Mid-, or Post-Tribulation*, Stanley N. Gundry, series editor, and Gleason L. Archer, general editor. Grand Rapids, MI: Zondervan, 1996.

Mowinckel, Sigmund. *He That Cometh: The Messiah Concept in the Old Testament and Later Judaism*. Translated by G. W. Anderson. Grand Rapids: Eerdmans, 2005.

Neusner, Jacob. *A Rabbi Talks with Jesus*. Montreal: McGill-Queen's University Press, 2001.

_____, ed. in chief. *Dictionary of Judaism in the Biblical Period: 450 BCE to 600 CE*, edited by William Scott Green. Peabody, Mass: Hendrickson, 1999.

_____. *The Talmud: What it is and What it Says*. Maryland: Rowan and

Littlefield, 2006. http://books.google.co.il/books?id=xKi6SLzfc KMC&print sec=frontcover&dq=Talmud&hl=en&ei=JVAwTM6 RNMe OjAfGzPHDBQ&sa=X&oi=book_result&ct=result&resnum =5&ved=0CEIQ6AEwBA#v=onepage&q&f=false (accessed July 6, 2010).

Nicklesburg, George W. E. *Resurrection, Immortality, and Eternal Life in Intertestamental Judaism and Early Christianity*, Harvard Theological Studies 56. Cambridge, MA: Harvard Univ. Press, 2006.

Nigro, H. L. *Before God's Wrath: The Bible's Answer to the Timing of the Rapture*. Milesburg, PA: Strong Tower Publishing, 2004.

Open Doors, *World Watch List 2018*, https://www.opendoorsusa.org/ christian-persecution/world-watch-list/ (accessed September 20, 2018).

Osborne, Grant R. "Revelation" in *Baker Exegetical Commentary on the NT*. Grand Rapids, MI: Baker Academic, 2002.

Patai, Raphael. *The Messiah Texts*. NY: Avon Books, 1979.

Payne, J. Barton. *Encyclopedia of Biblical Prophecy*. New York: Harper & Row, 1973.

Pentecost, Dwight J. *Eventos del Porvenir* (Spanish trans. of "Things to Come"). Deerfield, FL: Zondervan, 1977.

_____. *Profecías para el Mundo Moderno* (Spanish trans. of "Prophecy for Today"). Barcelona, Spain: Jorge Casas, 1973.

Pharr, W. Larry. *The Rapture Examined, Explained and Exposed.* USA: Xulon Press, 2007.

Rasmussen Reports, http://www.rasmussenreports.com/public_content/politics /general_politics/february_2017/democrats_think_muslims_worse_off_here_than_christians_are_in_muslim_world (accessed September 20, 2018).

Reddish, Mitchell G. *Apocalyptic Literature: A Reader.* Peabody, Mass: Hendrickson, 1990.

Reese, Alexander. *The Approaching Advent of Christ.* Grand Rapids, MI: International Publications Edition: 1975. (First print London: Marshall, Morgan, and Scott, 1937.)

Reiter, Richard R. "A History of the Development of the Rapture Positions" in *Three Views on The Rapture: Pre-, Mid-, or Post-Tribulation,* Stanley N. Gundry, series editor, and Gleason L. Archer, gen. ed. Grand Rapids, MI: Zondervan, 1996.

Rosenthal, Marvin. *The Pre-Wrath Rapture of the Church.* Nashville, TN: World Publ., 1990.

Saucy, Robert L. "The Eschatology of the Bible," Introductory Articles, Vol. 1 in *The Expositor's Bible Commentary*, Edited by Frank E. Gaebelein. Grand Rapids: Zondervan, 1979.

Schwartz, Leon. *Solid Foundations: A Post-Tribulation View of the End.* Columbia, SC: Self-published, 2018.

Scott, J. Julius, Jr. *Jewish Backgrounds of the New Testament*. Grand Rapids: Baker, 1995.

Sevener, Harold A. *Israel's Glorious Future: The Prophecies and Promises of God Revealed*. Charlotte, NC: Chosen People Ministries, 1996.

Shragai, Naday. *Turkey's Target: The Temple Mount*, Israel Hayom, https://www. israelhayom.com/opinions/turkeys-target-the-temple-mount/ (Accessed July 10, 2019).

Sim, David C. *Apocalyptic Eschatology in the Gospel of Matthew*. Brisbane, Australia: Cambridge, 1996.

Skarsaune, Oskar. "Fragments of Jewish Christian Literature Quoted in Some Greek and Latin Fathers" in *Jewish Believers in Jesus: The Early Centuries*, edited by Oskar Skarsaune and Reidar Hvalvik. Peabody, Mass: Hendrickson Publ., 2007.

Strong, James. *The New Strong's Expanded Dictionary of Bible Words*. Nashville, TN: Thomas Nelson, 2001.

Talbert, Charles H. *The Apocalypse: A Reading of the Revelation of John*. Louisville, KY: Westminster John Knox, 1994.

Thayer, Joseph H. *Thayer's Greek-English Lexicon of the New Testament*. Peabody, Mass: Hendrickson, 2009.

The Complete Artscroll Siddur, Weekly, Sabbath, Festival (Nusach Ashkenazi).

Translated by Rabbi Nosson Scherman, 2nd ed. New York: Mesorah Publ. Ltd, 1998.

The Preterist Archive, excerpted from "The Incredible Cover-up" by Dave MacPherson (1975), 171-176. https://www.preteristarchive. com/dEmEn TiA/1975_macpherson_incredible-coverup.html (accessed 3/13/19).

Towns, Elmer L. *Theology for Today*. Belmont, CA: Wadsworth, 2002.

Tregelles, Samuel Prideaux. *The Hope of Christ's Second Coming* (6th ed., with appendix by C. Y. Biss). England: Witstable Litho, 1886. https://redis covering thebible.com/ Tregelles1.pdf (accessed January 22, 2019).

United States Commission on International Religious Freedom, *US International Religious Freedom Report*, 47, https://www.uscirf. gov/reports-briefs/annual-report/2018-annual-report (accessed December 15, 2018).

Virkler, Henry A. *Hermeneutics: Principles and Processes of Biblical Interpretation*. Grand Rapids, MI: Baker Books, 1981.

Wagner, Clarence H. Jr., *Lessons from the Land of the Bible*. Jerusalem, Israel: Faith Publishing, 1998. http://www.ldolphin.org/replacement/ (accessed August 19, 2018).

Walls, Jerry L, Ed. *The Oxford Handbook of Eschatology*. New York, NY: Oxford Univ. Press, 2008.

Walvoord, John F. *Revelation*. Chicago, Illinois: Moody Publishers, 2011.

_____. *The Rapture Question*. Grand Rapids, MI: Zondervan Publ. House, 1979.

_____. "Unresolved Problems of Posttribulationism" in *Posttribula-tionism Today*, https://bible.org/series/posttribulationism-today (accessed September 1, 2018).

Weinthal, Benjamin. *Call to Destroy Israel at Islamist Conference in Ankara*, The Jerusalem Post, https://www.jpost.com/Arab-Israeli-Conflict/Call-to-destroy-Israel-at-Islamist-conference-in-Ankara-602442, (Accessed September 23, 2019).

Wheeler, Scott A. *Here Till the End.* Columbia, SC: Self-published, 2018.

Woodridge, Charles J. *Bible Prophecy Study Guide*. Chicago, IL: Moody Bile Institute Center for External Studies, 1994.

World Watch Monitor, *Iran: Staggering Number of Christians Arrested – 114 in a Week*, https://www. worldwatch monitor.org/2018/12/iran-staggering-number-of-christians-arrested-114-in-a-week/ (accessed 12/5/18).

Wright, N. T. "Christian Origins and the Resurrection of Jesus: The Resurrection of Jesus as a Historical Problem" in *Theological Review*, 41.2, 1988, http://www.ntwrightpage.com/Wright_Historical_Problem.htm (accessed March 17, 2011).

_____. *Paul for Everyone: Galatians and Thessalonians.* Louisville, KY: Westminster John Knox Press, 2004.

Yalon, Yori. *Turkish Organization teaches Arab kids from East Jerusalem that Israel is theirs.* Israel Hayom, https://www.israelhayom.com/2019/07/09/turkish-organization-teaches-arab-kids-from-east-jerusalem-that-israel-is-theirs/ (Accessed July 10, 2019).S

Printed in the United States
By Bookmasters